INFORMATION POWER

BUILDING PARTNERSHIPS FOR LEARNING

Prepared by the
American Association of School Librarians

Association for Educational Communications
and Technology

American Library Association
Chicago and London

1998

The paper used in this publication meets the minimum requirements of American National Standard Information Sciences—Permanence of Paper for Printed Library Materials, ANSI Z39.48-1992. ∞

Library of Congress Cataloging-in-Publication Data
American Association of School Librarians.
Information power : building partnerships for learning / prepared by the American Association of School Librarians [and] Association for Educational Communications and Technology.
    p.   cm.
Includes bibliographical references and index.
ISBN 0-8389-3470-6 (paper)
    1. School libraries—United States.   2. Instructional materials centers—United States.   3. Library orientation for school children—United States.   I. Association for Educational Communications and Technology.   II. Title.
Z675.S3A4475   1998   98-23291
027.8'0973—dc21   CIP

07   06   7   6

Contents

Preface

A t the end of the second millennium, school library media service has undergone a radical change in emphasis. The focus of school library media programs has moved from resources to students to creating a community of lifelong learners. Students and their learning remain at the core of library media programs and services, shaping the functions of school library media specialists. Effective teaching is today seen as a holistic process involving all aspects of student life and requiring continual assessment and feedback for meaningful learning.

This change in emphasis is reflected in this new edition, now entitled *Information Power: Building Partnerships for Learning,* which includes information literacy standards for student learning as well. The standards themselves are also available in a separate publication, entitled *Information Literacy Standards for Student Learning,* which can be distributed to our partners in learning—classroom teachers, school administrators, parents, and other community members. *Information Power* and the *Standards* were developed jointly over a three-year period by the American Association of School Librarians (AASL) and the Association for Educational Communications and Technology (AECT).

Information Power

Information Power: Building Partnerships for Learning builds upon a long history of guidelines published by the American Library Association to foster improvement in school library media programs. Just as the philosophical direction of the guidelines has changed, so has the presentation of the guidelines themselves.

In 1920, the National Education Association's Committee on Library Organization and Equipment published standards for senior and junior high schools. These were followed by the 1925 *Elementary School Library Standards* (a joint NEA and ALA publication, also published by ALA).

The first set of national K–12 school library standards, *School Libraries for Today and Tomorrow,* published in 1945, became the precedent for today's school library media programs. They differentiated between the school librarian and the public librarian and defined the different service functions that the school library and the public library provided to schools.

Standards for School Library Programs, prepared by the American Association of School Librarians, was published in 1960. These standards addressed changes since 1945, including the significant shift in the school librarian's role, which by 1960 emphasized serving students and teachers with direct student services that centered on enriching their personal and instructional activities. Besides urging that school librarians work closely with teachers in selection and use of all types of learning materials, the standards emphasized the school librarian's role as a teacher who was jointly responsible with the classroom teacher for teaching library skills as an integrated part of the classroom instruction.

Standards for School Media Programs, prepared by AASL and the Department of Audiovisual Instruction of the National Education Association (DAVI, now AECT) in cooperation with several other national associations, was published in 1969. The name of the standards, the joint authorship, and the use of such terms as *media* and *media specialist* emphasized the broad focus of the school library media program by that time. The school library media specialist's role included working with students to help them develop competence in listening, viewing, and reading skills.

In 1975 *Media Programs: District and School* was published as a collaborative effort of AASL and AECT. These standards reflected the influence of a systems approach to media services. *Media Programs: District and School* also provided sets of "guiding principles" to aid in local program decisions as well as standards.

The 1988 publication of *Information Power: Guidelines for School Library Media Programs* saw the continuance of AASL and AECT's collaborative efforts. Significant changes within education and expanded access to new sources of information brought local professionals into new areas of decision-making as they broadened the access to and use of information by students, teachers, and parents.

Information Power and *Information Literacy Standards*

Profound changes in society and technology during the past decade have resulted in massive changes in education and school library media programs. Children and young people still look to their schools for information beyond academics, but the explosion of knowledge made possible by advances in information technology has given the schools and their library media programs more options for responding to this goal. The content of knowledge and the ways of accessing it continue to grow exponentially.

Information Power approaches this twofold growth by advocating the creation of a community of lifelong learners. Information literacy —understanding how to access and use information—is at the core of lifelong learning. Rather than a situation-specific document, the new *Information Power* provides broad guidelines, with some helpful examples, for local professionals to adapt to their individual learning situations within their school library media programs.

In the collaborative effort to revise the 1988 edition of *Information Power,* AASL and AECT expanded the concept of the book to include the opportunity to have separate access to the standards discussed in the book itself. This edition of *Information Power* now includes a supplemental companion volume, entitled *Information Literacy Standards for Student Learning,* which contains just the standards themselves along with chapter 1, The Vision. School library media specialists and teachers can distribute the *Standards* to their partners in learning so that these important participants can take a more active part in the learning process that the book develops. *Information Power* provides the strategies for building the foundation for learning; the *Standards* gives library media specialists an opportunity to extend the framework for that foundation into their communities.

Many people in the profession were involved in the 1998 *Information Power* project, devoting countless hours to developing the Standards and the *Information Power* manuscript, and many state associations and individuals donated funds for the writing project. Many members of both boards and many leaders of AASL and AECT worked to refine the documents. The Vision Committee and its chair deserve special recognition for their contribution to the project, as does the project writer for creating the original manuscript. All contributors are listed in appendix F.

We look forward to the challenges before us and trust that *Information Power: Building Partnerships for Learning* and its companion volume, *Information Literacy Standards for Student Learning,* will once again be part of your program's ongoing success.

Ken Haycock, AASL President
Robert A. Harrell, AECT President

Introduction

nformation Power: Building Partnerships for Learning represents a powerful tool that library media specialists can use to foster the active, authentic learning that today's researchers and practitioners recognize as vital to helping students become independent, information-literate, lifelong learners. Its content provides a conceptual foundation that school library media specialists can adapt and apply to their own circumstances, local programs, and activities. *Information Power* is written at a general level so that library media specialists and others in individual states, districts, and sites can tailor its ideas to meet local needs.

Information Power: Building Partnerships for Learning is built upon a set of nine information literacy standards designed to guide and support library media specialists' efforts in the three major areas:

Learning and teaching

Information access

Program administration

Information Power also shows how skills and strategies in collaboration, leadership, and technology support these efforts. It stresses the importance of making connections to the learning community of the twenty-first century as the school library media program develops the fundamentals of lifelong learning in students.

Part One

Chapter 1, The Vision, begins with the vision behind both *Information Power* and the standards. It contains the philosophy statement for the standards, followed by the mission and goals of the school library media program. Chapter 2, Information Literacy Standards for Student Learning, presents the standards themselves, which provide a conceptual framework and broad guidelines for describing the information-literate student.

The standards consist of three categories, nine standards, and twenty-nine indicators. The core learning outcomes that are most directly related to the services provided by school library media programs are found in the three standards and thirteen indicators in the "information literacy" category. The other two categories—three standards and seven indicators for "independent learning" and three standards and nine indicators for "social responsibility"—are grounded in information literacy but describe more general aspects of student learning to which school library media programs also make important contributions. Taken together, the categories, standards, and indicators describe the content and processes related to information that students must master to be considered information literate.

The pattern of organization includes, first, a paragraph explaining the standard that is followed by a list of its associated indicators. This general introduction provides a brief overview of the standard, its meaning, and the ways its achievement can be assessed. A box follows each indicator to show how it applies to students. Three "Levels of Proficiency" descriptors follow each indicator to assist in gauging the extent to which individual students have mastered the components of information literacy. These items, like the standards and indicators themselves, are written at a general level to allow local teachers and library media specialists full flexibility in determining the amount and kind of detail that should structure student evaluations.

Next, four sample information problems appear under the heading, "Standards in Action." These problems illustrate potential situations in which information, used appropriately and efficiently, is needed to solve a problem specific to the given standard. Across the document, problems were selected and created by practicing library media specialists to show how the standards relate to all four of the major student groups (K–2, 3–5, 6–8, and 9–12) and to all areas of the curriculum. Although a specific curricular area is indicated for each problem, this information merely suggests a focus for the related activity: most, if not all, of the problems are cross-curricular and can be used to help students achieve a variety of subject-matter objectives.

Finally, examples of indicators for content-area standards developed by various national groups in such content areas as history, mathematics, etc., illustrate the integral relationship of the standard to students' learning across the curriculum. By highlighting some of these links, this segment provides a tool for library media specialists and teachers to use as they collaboratively design learning experiences that will help students master both disciplinary content and information literacy.

The standards and indicators themselves were reviewed by members of the field and other educators at various points in their development. Throughout the project, comments and suggestions from a wide range of practitioners and others were collected electronically, through face-to-face conversations, and in formal hearings held at AASL and AECT conferences. During 1996–97, a panel of fifty-seven educators within and beyond the school library media field participated in a national Delphi study designed to provide a formal validation of the items. Panelists reacted to an early draft of all the statements, both the standards and the indicators, over the first three rounds of the study. After the statements had been revised on the basis of the panelists' and others' suggestions, the panel assessed the revised versions of the statements in a fourth and final Delphi round. The list published here reflects insights and suggestions from all those who participated in this extensive reviewing process.

The "Levels of Proficiency" that follow each indicator are based on a variety of sources and are designed to reflect the levels of learning outlined in Bloom *et al., A Taxonomy of Educational Objectives: Handbook I. The Cognitive Domain,* in order to show how students can build from a beginning awareness of information literacy to a more complex understanding. The progression implied in the items' sequencing ("basic," "proficient," "exemplary") does not correspond exactly to developmental levels, but it does suggest that items for each indicator can be designed for elementary, middle-school, and high-school students. An appendix provides information about assessment guidelines and examples.

The content-area standards were extracted from Kendall and Marzano's *Content Knowledge: A Compendium of Standards and Benchmarks for K–12 Education,* 2nd ed. This document was originally compiled by the Midcontinent Research and Evaluation Laboratory, known as McREL, and the indicators are identified in the text in connection with their associated McREL Standards. Within this document, the content-area standards are presented verbatim from the Kendall and Marzano text. As a result, they reflect the different approaches of the different national standards-writing groups represented in that text and vary considerably in their language and their levels of detail.

Each information literacy standard is accompanied by one indicator from each content area for which there is at least one clearly relevant link. Over eighty content-area indicators were selected to show as closely as possible the links between information literacy and fourteen content areas. Some standards and content areas share many explicit links—for example, the standards related to creative expression and the content covered by the Arts Standards and the English Language Arts Standards—but other relationships are less apparent. Information literacy underlies student learning in all the content areas, but its relationship to individual content-area outcomes is often implicit rather than obvious. Library media specialists and teachers—working together to plan, conduct, and evaluate instruction—must look beyond the individual statements in order to interpret the links and to mesh them with their own local curricula and student needs.

Another set of learning outcomes—the Schoolwide Goals for Student Learning—are included as an appendix for reference. These Goals were jointly developed in 1996 by the National Study of School Evaluation and the Alliance for Curriculum Reform. The statements are not content-area standards but descriptions of outcomes that are more general in nature and focus. Many of them are directly related to the information literacy standards for student learning and provide yet another tool for teachers and library media specialists to use in linking information literacy and the other kinds of learning that students will need in the twenty-first century.

Information literacy is basic to student learning, and the outcomes described in chapter 2, Information Literacy Standards for Student Learning, are basic to student mastery of the concepts and skills that citizens will need in the information age. The student who works at all these outcomes throughout a school career will emerge as an information-literate high school graduate: one who has the ability to use information to acquire basic and advanced knowledge; to become an independent, lifelong learner; and to contribute effectively and responsibly to the learning community.

Library media specialists may want to share these information literacy standards with their partners in learning, such as classroom teachers, school administrators, parents and other community members. To facilitate that objective, these first two chapters have been reproduced as a separate publication entitled *Information Literacy Standards for Student Learning*.

Part Two

Part Two begins with chapter 3, Collaboration, Leadership, and Technology, which introduces and discusses the three unifying themes—collaboration, leadership, and technology—that underlie the vision of library media programs presented here. These themes weave through the subsequent chapters to show how they relate to each component of the library media program.

Chapters 4, 5, and 6 cover the school library media program's primary responsibilities of Learning and Teaching, Information Access and Delivery, and Program Administration, respectively. These three chapters are structured around a series of twenty-seven principles. Identified by the Vision Committee, disseminated for review and comment in the field, and approved by the AASL and AECT Boards, these principles are the cardinal premises on which the effective school library media program is based. As guidelines rather than prescriptions, the principles support and enrich the work of individual school library media programs and specialists rather than impose specific activities.

Each principle in chapters 4, 5, and 6 is followed by supporting text. The text relates the principle to the library media program and presents the implications of the principle for the school library media specialist. A series of goals for the school library media specialist follow each principle. These three chapters also show collaboration, leadership, and technology as key to effective learning and teaching, information access, and program administration. Taken as a whole, the principles and their supporting text paint a comprehensive picture of the dynamic, effective, student-centered library media program. The discussion for individual principles is brief and can stand alone, allowing the school library media specialist to refer to the principles quickly and readily and to present them succinctly to others, especially in discussions of the library media program's role and requirements. Each segment collapses its content into only a few paragraphs, allowing the library media specialist to build on it with details and suggestions in local contexts and issues.

Chapter 7, Connections to the Learning Community, explores how the school library media specialist can initiate and foster connections into the learning community beyond the confines of the individual program and school. The learning community begins with the student at the center and moves outward to include the school; family and local resources; district, state, and regional agencies; professional associations and national resources; and international and global resources. This final chapter shows how using collaboration, leadership, and technology strategies to make connections throughout the learning community helps the school library media specialist develop students' lifelong learning skills that will be essential to thriving in the twenty-first century.

Selected references with brief annotations appear at the end of chapters 2 through 7. These resources support the ideas discussed in each chapter. It should be noted that the lists are by no means exhaustive.

The appendixes at the end of *Information Power* provide further helpful information for school library media specialists. The appendixes include Library Power, ICONnect, ALA and AECT Statements and Policies, the National Study of School Evaluation Schoolwide Goals for Student Learning, Student Performance Assessment, and Contributors. As with the previous edition of *Information Power* and earlier published standards documents, it is also anticipated that more supporting documents will soon be available to help implement *Information Power* and the standards.

Implementing the information literacy standards for student learning in the school library media program can help it develop the concepts, attitudes, and skills in students that will be essential in the coming years. The school library media specialist who uses the themes of collaboration, leadership, and technology in applying the principles of *Information Power: Building Partnerships for Learning* will help students and others become full and productive members of the learning community—the ultimate goal of the school library media program.

PART ONE

INFORMATION LITERACY STANDARDS FOR STUDENT LEARNING

Chapter 1

The Vision

Information literacy—the ability to find and use information—is the keystone of lifelong learning. Creating a foundation for lifelong learning is at the heart of the school library media program. Just as the school library media center has moved far beyond a room with books to become an active, technology-rich learning environment with an array of information resources, the school library media specialist today focuses on the process of learning rather than dissemination of information. The library media program combines effective learning and teaching strategies and activities with information access skills. Information availability will undoubtedly continue to mushroom into the next century, which will make a strong school library media program even more essential to help its users acquire the skills they will need to harness and use information for a productive and fulfilling life.

The school library media specialist can use the information literacy standards for student learning to create and maintain a program for a broad learning community—students, teachers, administrators, parents, and the neighborhood—that will support lifelong learning. The philosophy statement of the standards follows; a mission and goals statement also appears below.

PHILOSOPHY

Today's student lives and learns in a world that has been radically altered by the ready availability of vast stores of information in a variety of formats. Innovations in traditional printing techniques have joined with advances in electronic technologies to transform the ways we seek and gain information. Students now routinely encounter information in formats as simple as the picture book, as complex as the multimedia package, and as diverse as the literary classic and the personal homepage. The information explosion has provided countless opportunities for students and has dramatically altered the knowledge and abilities they will need to live productively in the twenty-first century. Students must become skillful consumers and producers of information in a range of sources and formats to thrive personally and economically in the communication age. Library media programs must be dynamic, enthusiastic, and student centered to help ensure that all students achieve this status.

Contemporary learning theory describes the student as an active and engaged information user and underscores the importance of students' developing information expertise. Cognitive psychologists define learning itself as the active building of knowledge through dynamic interaction with information and experience. Theorists in the information field contend that the information search process mirrors this description of the learning process: students actively seek to construct meaning from the sources they encounter and to create products that shape and communicate that meaning effectively. Core elements in both learning and information theory thus converge to suggest that developing expertise in accessing, evaluating, and using information is in fact the authentic learning that modern education seeks to promote.

Promoting authentic learning demands both an acceptance of current learning and information theory and a new conception of the context of education. For all students, that context will include learning environments that are fundamentally different from any that we have known. Central to this new context is the idea of the "learning community." This phrase suggests that all of us—students, teachers, administrators, and parents as well as our local, regional, state, national, and international communities—are interconnected in a lifelong quest to understand and meet our constantly changing information needs. This new learning community is not limited by time, place, age, occupation, or disciplinary borders but instead is linked by interest, need, and a growing array of telecommunications technology.

Helping students flourish in this learning community is the central concern of student-centered library media programs. The goal is to assist all students in becoming active and creative locators, evaluators, and users of information to solve problems and to satisfy their own curiosity. With these abilities, students can become independent, ethical, lifelong learners who achieve personal satisfaction and who contribute responsibly and productively to the learning community and to society as a whole.

Library media specialists have always drawn upon a distinctive expertise about information, and a growing body of research is demonstrating the unique contribution this expertise can bring to student achievement. The library media specialist's mastery has traditionally encompassed a wide range of information formats as well as a sensitivity to the information needs of a wide range of audiences. Especially in recent years, the profession has pioneered in identifying and meeting learning needs brought about by the rapid and continuing expansion of information delivered through a variety of new technologies. Now, as the keystone of a student-centered library media program, the library media specialist is poised to work collaboratively with teachers, administrators, and others to facilitate students' entry into the communication age. As an essential partner who both contributes to and draws from the expertise of the entire learning community, the library media specialist plays a role that

- begins with promoting and reinforcing students' interests and abilities in reading, listening, and viewing
- expands to include fostering the full range of information concepts, strategies, and abilities students must master to profit from the global resources that are quite literally at their fingertips
- includes developing the full range of abilities that students need to interact effectively with information and to construct meaningful knowledge:
  - analyzing complex and conflicting presentations of information
  - appreciating the variety of perspectives offered by individual viewpoints, scholarly disciplines, and cultural understandings
  - using information competently in critical thinking, decision making, and problem solving
  - producing new information and creating products and presentations that communicate ideas efficiently and effectively
  - acting responsibly in regard to information, particularly with respect to the difficult issues of intellectual freedom, equitable access to information, and intellectual property rights in an age of global interconnectivity

— developing into lifelong learners who can assimilate varying viewpoints, accommodate change, and contribute to the well-being of the community.

As the essential link who connects students, teachers, and others with the information resources they need, the library media specialist plays a unique and pivotal role in the learning community. To fulfill this role, the effective library media specialist draws upon a vision for the student-centered library media program that is based on three central ideas: collaboration, leadership, and technology. These ideas underlie the vision presented in the information literacy standards and provide unifying themes for guiding the library media specialist and the library media program. They are interwoven throughout the following descriptions of the library media specialist's specific responsibilities:

- As teacher, the library media specialist collaborates with students and other members of the learning community to analyze learning and information needs, to locate and use resources that will meet those needs, and to understand and communicate the information the resources provide. An effective instructor of students, the library media specialist is knowledgeable about current research on teaching and learning and skilled in applying its findings to a variety of situations—particularly those that call upon students to access, evaluate, and use information from multiple sources in order to learn, to think, and to create and apply new knowledge. A curricular leader and a full participant on the instructional team, the library media specialist constantly updates personal skills and knowledge in order to work effectively with teachers, administrators, and other staff—both to expand their general understanding of information issues and to provide them with specific opportunities to develop sophisticated skills in information literacy, including the uses of information technology.

- As instructional partner, the library media specialist joins with teachers and others to identify links across student information needs, curricular content, learning outcomes, and a wide variety of print, nonprint, and electronic information resources. Working with the entire school community, the library media specialist takes a leading role in developing policies, practices, and curricula that guide students to develop the full range of information and communication abilities. Committed to the process of collaboration, the library media specialist works closely with individual teachers in the critical areas of designing authentic learning tasks and assessments and integrating the information and communication abilities required to meet subject matter standards.

- As information specialist, the library media specialist provides leadership and expertise in acquiring and evaluating information resources in all formats; in bringing an awareness of information issues into collaborative relationships with teachers, administrators, students, and others; and in modeling for students and others strategies for locating, accessing, and evaluating information within and beyond the library media center. Working in an environment that has been profoundly affected by technology, the library media specialist both masters sophisticated electronic resources and maintains a constant focus on the nature, quality, and ethical uses of information available in these and in more traditional tools.

- As program administrator, the library media specialist works collaboratively with members of the learning community to define the policies of the library media program and to guide and direct all the activities related to it. Confident of the importance of the effective use of information and information technology to students' personal and economic success in their future lives, the library media specialist is an advocate for the library media program and provides the knowledge, vision, and leadership to steer it creatively and energetically in the twenty-first century. Proficient in the management of staff, budgets, equipment, and facilities, the library media specialist plans, executes, and evaluates the program to ensure its quality both at a general level and on a day-to-day basis.

Issues related to information and communication have long been the concern of the library media specialist and the library media field. Drawing upon contemporary understandings as well as the field's traditional emphasis on the critical evaluation and use of information, the library media specialist plays a unique and vital role in helping students, teachers, and other school and community leaders develop the knowledge, abilities, and attitudes that are crucial to the broader learning community in the communication age.

MISSION AND GOALS OF THE SCHOOL LIBRARY MEDIA PROGRAM

The mission of the library media program is to ensure that students and staff are effective users of ideas and information. This mission is accomplished:

- by providing intellectual and physical access to materials in all formats
- by providing instruction to foster competence and stimulate interest in reading, viewing, and using information and ideas
- by working with other educators to design learning strategies to meet the needs of individual students.

This didn't change, but for me, the mission did from 1988 to 1998.

—*Information Power: Guidelines for School Library Media Programs* (1988), p. 1

The mission statement for *Information Power: Guidelines for School Library Media Programs* is as relevant today as it was in 1988, and so it remains the mission statement for the information literacy standards for student learning as well as for *Information Power: Building Partnerships for Learning.* Although changes in society, education, and technology have transformed many of the challenges facing library media programs during the past decade, the mission itself remains the same. Today, this mission focuses on offering programs and services that are centered on information literacy and that are designed around active, authentic student learning as described in the information literacy standards for student learning. The goals of today's library media program point to the development of a community of learners that is centered on the student and sustained by a creative, energetic library media program. These goals are as follows:

1. To provide intellectual access to information through learning activities that are integrated into the curriculum and that help all students achieve information literacy by developing effective cognitive strategies for selecting, retrieving, analyzing, evaluating, synthesizing, creating, and communicating information in all formats and in all content areas of the curriculum

2. To provide physical access to information through

   a. a carefully selected and systematically organized local collection of diverse learning resources that represent a wide range of subjects, levels of difficulty, and formats;

   b. a systematic procedure for acquiring information and materials from outside the library media center and the school through such mechanisms as electronic networks, interlibrary loan, and cooperative agreements with other information agencies; and instruction in using a range of equipment for accessing local and remote information in any format

3. To provide learning experiences that encourage students and others to become discriminating consumers and skilled creators of information through comprehensive instruction related to the full range of communications media and technology

4. To provide leadership, collaboration, and assistance to teachers and others in applying principles of instructional design to the use of instructional and information technology for learning

5. To provide resources and activities that contribute to lifelong learning while accommodating a wide range of differences in teaching and learning styles, methods, interests, and capacities

6. To provide a program that functions as the information center of the school, both through offering a locus for integrated and interdisciplinary learning activities within the school and through offering access to a full range of information for learning beyond this locus

7. To provide resources and activities for learning that represent a diversity of experiences, opinions, and social and cultural perspectives and to support the concept that intellectual freedom and access to information are prerequisite to effective and responsible citizenship in a democracy.

Chapter 2

Information Literacy Standards for Student Learning

The information literacy standards for student learning and the indicators for each standard were developed with the following supporting material:

- *Levels of Proficiency* items for the indicators within each standard
- *Standards in Action* that provide examples of potential situations requiring information literacy for each standard
- *Examples of Content-Area Standards* for each standard

The supporting material is provided to illustrate how the standards and indicators can be applied. The samples should be interpreted and modified in view of individual learning tasks and goals.

THE NINE INFORMATION LITERACY STANDARDS FOR STUDENT LEARNING

Information Literacy

Standard 1: The student who is information literate accesses information efficiently and effectively.

Standard 2: The student who is information literate evaluates information critically and competently.

Standard 3: The student who is information literate uses information accurately and creatively.

Independent Learning

Standard 4: The student who is an independent learner is information literate and pursues information related to personal interests.

Standard 5: The student who is an independent learner is information literate and appreciates literature and other creative expressions of information.

> Standard 6: The student who is an independent learner is information literate and strives for excellence in information seeking and knowledge generation.
>
> **Social Responsibility**
> Standard 7: The student who contributes positively to the learning community and to society is information literate and recognizes the importance of information to a democratic society.
>
> Standard 8: The student who contributes positively to the learning community and to society is information literate and practices ethical behavior in regard to information and information technology.
>
> Standard 9: The student who contributes positively to the learning community and to society is information literate and participates effectively in groups to pursue and generate information.

INFORMATION LITERACY STANDARDS

Standard 1   The student who is information literate accesses information efficiently and effectively.

The student who is information literate recognizes that having good information is central to meeting the opportunities and challenges of day-to-day living. That student knows when to seek information beyond his or her personal knowledge, how to frame questions that will lead to the appropriate information, and where to seek that information. The student knows how to structure a search across a variety of sources and formats to locate the best information to meet a particular need.

Indicators

Indicator 1. Recognizes the need for information

Levels of Proficiency

Basic Gives examples of situations in which additional information (beyond one's own knowledge) is needed to resolve an information problem or question.

Proficient When faced with an information problem or question, determines whether additional information (beyond one's own knowledge) is needed to resolve it.

Exemplary Assesses whether a range of information problems or questions can be resolved based on one's own knowledge or whether additional information is required.

> Students' overview of a topic or issue demonstrates their understanding of how an idea connects to other ideas as well as other issues that may be involved in the main issue.

Indicator 2. Recognizes that accurate and comprehensive information is the basis for intelligent decision making

Levels of Proficiency

Basic Selects examples of accurate and inaccurate information and of complete and incomplete information for decision making.

Proficient Explains the differences between accurate and inaccurate information and complete and incomplete information for decision making.

Exemplary Judges the quality of decisions in terms of the accuracy and completeness of the information on which they were based.

> Students understand there is information on more than one side of an issue and remain open to other perspectives; they also judge the completeness of their information before making a decision.

Indicator 3. Formulates questions based on information needs

Levels of Proficiency

Basic States at least one broad question that will help in finding needed information.

Proficient States both broad and specific questions that will help in finding needed information.

Exemplary Revises, adds, and deletes questions as information needs change.

Students change and refine their questions as their research proceeds by developing *essential questions* that go beyond simple fact-finding and that promote thoughtful interpretation, synthesis, and presentation of newly found knowledge.

Indicator 4. Identifies a variety of potential sources of information

Levels of Proficiency

Basic Lists several sources of information and explains the kind of information found in each.

Proficient Brainstorms a range of sources of information that will meet an information need.

Exemplary Uses a full range of information sources to meet differing information needs.

Students acquire strategies for locating a variety of formats to satisfy information needs, including print, nonprint, and electronic as well as human resources of varying points of view and depths of coverage, and they differentiate between primary and secondary sources.

Indicator 5. Develops and uses successful strategies for locating information

Levels of Proficiency

Basic Lists some ideas for how to identify and find needed information.

Proficient Explains and applies a plan to access needed information.

Exemplary Formulates and revises plans for accessing information for a range of needs and situations.

Students quickly and effectively locate the most relevant information for research questions within the sources they have gathered, and they vary their strategies according to the format, organization, and search capability of the source and according to the particular issue they are researching.

Standards in Action

Grades K–2 (Geography) Students visit the local airport and meet an aviator who plans to replicate and finish Amelia Earhart's attempted route around the world. The aviator explains that she has done extensive research and will follow Earhart's flight plan except for parts of Africa: she was unable to obtain permission to fly over some countries and has had to change the route slightly. The students log on to the Internet to follow the trip. They make a large map and track the flight. The students locate islands that are not in their classroom atlas.

Grades 3–5 (History) A fifth-grade class explores the culture and everyday lives of the early settlers of their state. Students formulate questions based on their own lives to learn how children lived in pioneer times. The class knows that the state encyclopedia has a great deal of information about the settlers, but the language is difficult and technical. Students discuss other resources that might have appropriate information.

Grades 6–8 (English Language Arts) A middle-school class reads Greek and Roman mythology and creates a book to illustrate contemporary uses of Greek and Roman mythological figures. The students look for references to ancient heroes in a variety of modern settings, such as ads for food and for other products and names of companies and businesses. In addition to producing examples of the uses—e.g., a picture of Mercury as the symbol for a delivery service—students do research to ascertain what particular attribute of a hero—e.g., speed—contributed to the company's choice of that hero as a symbol.

Grades 9–12 (Science) To stump their classmates in a "Chemistry Bowl," teams of Advanced Placement students identify chemical processes involved in making and using several everyday products. Students focus on science journals and technical books to identify a wide range of consumer products that involve unexpected chemicals and chemical processes.

Examples of Content-Area Standards

Content-area standards that can be linked to information literacy standard 1 include but are not limited to the following examples.

Behavioral Studies Understands that people can learn about others in many different ways (e.g., experience, mass communications media, conversations with others about their work and lives). Standard 1, Grades 3–5 Indicator (McREL, p. 591)

Civics Knows alternative ideas about the sources of law (e.g., custom, Supreme Being, sovereigns, legislatures) and different varieties of law (e.g., divine law, natural law, common law, statute law, international law). Standard 3, Grades 9–12 Indicator (McREL, p. 419)

English Language Arts Uses a variety of resource materials to gather information for research topics (e.g., magazines, newspapers, dictionaries, schedules, journals, phone directories, globes, atlases, almanacs). Standard 4, Grades 6–8 Indicator (McREL, p. 332)

Foreign Language Understands the content of ability-appropriate primary sources on familiar topics (e.g., personal letters, pamphlets, illustrated newspaper and magazine articles, advertisements). Standard 2, Grades 5–8 Indicator (McREL, p. 500)

Geography Knows the characteristics and purposes of geographic databases (e.g., databases containing census data, land-use data, topographic information). Standard 1, Grades 6–8 Indicator (McREL, p. 511)

Health Knows local, state, federal, and private agencies that protect and/or inform the consumer (e.g., FDA, EPA, OSHA, local prosecutor's office). Standard 1, Grades 9–12 Indicator (McREL, p. 546)

History Knows different types of primary and secondary sources and the motives, interests, and bias expressed in them (e.g., eyewitness accounts, letters, diaries, artifacts, photos, magazine articles, newspaper accounts, hearsay). Historical Understanding Standard 2, Grades 7–8 Indicator (McREL, pp. 113–114)

Life Skills Asks "how do you know" in appropriate situations. Thinking and Reasoning Standard 1, Grades K–2 Indicator (McREL, p. 607)

Mathematics Formulates a problem, determines information required to solve the problem, chooses methods for obtaining this information, and sets limits for acceptable solutions. Standard 1, Grades 6–8 Indicator (McREL, p. 47)

Science Knows that tools (e.g., thermometers, magnifiers, rulers, balances) can be used to gather information and extend the senses. Standard 15, Grades K–2 Indicator (McREL, p. 99)

Technology Knows the common features and uses of databases (e.g., databases contain records of similar data, which is sorted or organized for ease of use; databases are used in both print form, such as telephone books, and electronic form, such as computerized card catalogs). Standard 2, Grades 3–5 Indicator (McREL, p. 581)

Standard 2   The student who is information literate evaluates information critically and competently.

The student who is information literate weighs information carefully and wisely to determine its quality. That student understands traditional and emerging principles for assessing the accuracy, validity, relevance, completeness, and impartiality of information. The student applies these principles insightfully across information sources and formats and uses logic and informed judgment to accept, reject, or replace information to meet a particular need.

Indicators

Indicator 1. Determines accuracy, relevance, and comprehensiveness

Levels of Proficiency

Basic Defines or gives examples of the terms "accuracy," "relevance," and "comprehensiveness."

Proficient Compares and contrasts sources related to a topic to determine which are more accurate, relevant, and comprehensive.

Exemplary Judges the accuracy, relevance, and completeness of sources and information in relation to a range of topics and information problems.

> Students realize they will find conflicting facts in different sources, and they determine the accuracy and relevance of information before taking notes. They determine the adequacy of information gathered according to the complexity of the topic, the research questions, and the product that is expected.

Indicator 2. Distinguishes among fact, point of view, and opinion

Levels of Proficiency

Basic Recognizes fact, opinion, and point of view in various information sources and products.

Proficient Explains how fact, point of view, and opinion are different from one another.

Exemplary Assembles facts, opinions, and point of view as appropriate in one's own work.

> Students know when facts must be used, when opinions can be used, and how the validity of opinions can be verified. They determine how different points of view can influence the facts and opinions presented in controversial issues.

Indicator 3. Identifies inaccurate and misleading information

Levels of Proficiency

Basic Recognizes inaccurate or misleading information in information sources and products.

Proficient Explains why inaccurate and misleading information can lead to faulty conclusions.

Exemplary Judges and supports judgments of the degree of inaccuracy, bias, or misleading information in information sources and products.

> Students differentiate between misinterpreted or misstated facts and inaccuracies that are based on opinion, they can identify inaccuracies caused by leaving out or slanting information, and they determine inaccuracies by gathering and comparing information from a wide range of sources.

Indicator 4. Selects information appropriate to the problem or question at hand

Levels of Proficiency

Basic Recognizes information that is applicable to a specific information problem or question.

Proficient Analyzes information from a variety of sources to determine its applicability to a specific information problem or question.

Exemplary Integrates accurate, relevant, and comprehensive information to resolve an information problem or question.

> Students continually assess research questions and problems, and they select the main ideas and supporting details that accurately and comprehensively meet their specific information needs. They revise their topics and their search strategies as they uncover information that may not fit with previous knowledge or that offers a new direction on their topics.

Standards in Action

Grades K–2 (Mathematics) Students who are learning the alphabet have just discovered the many kinds of alphabet books in the library media center. They make a pictograph showing what they learn from these books: how many use drawings to show the letters, how many use photographs, how many use paintings, and how many tell stories.

Grades 3–5 (Science) A fourth-grade class researches endangered animals. The students use books, CD-ROMs, and the Internet to gather information. One group notices that a particular homepage has more dire predictions than other sources about the future of their animal. Checking more closely, the group finds that the host of the homepage is an environmentalist organization known for its aggressive viewpoint. Students wonder whether to accept the information as valid.

Grades 6–8 (Arts) An art class collaborates with a history class to create a "museum display" about the City of Jerusalem. Small groups research various facets of the city—its ancient and recent history; its status as a holy city for three major religious groups; and the contributions each of these groups has made to the art, architecture, and culture of the present city.

Grades 9–12 (English Language Arts) Students need to identify a person living today who meets the literary definition of a tragic hero and to find information to support their choices. As a class, students develop a rubric to identify the essential traits of a tragic hero and to specify the kind and amount of evidence required to "certify" someone as a contemporary tragic hero. After using biographical information to begin a list of potential tragic heroes, students explore a wide range of other resources to amass as much authoritative evidence as possible to support their choices. The class judges each case against the rubric.

Examples of Content-Area Standards

Content-area standards that can be linked to information literacy standard 2 include but are not limited to the following examples.

Art Connections Understands how elements, materials, technologies, artistic processes (e.g., imagination, craftsmanship), and organizational principles (e.g., unity and variety, repetition and contrast) are used in similar and distinctive ways in the various art forms. Standard 1, Grades 9–12 Indicator (McREL, p. 381)

Civics Knows how to use criteria such as logical validity, factual accuracy, emotional appeal, distorted evidence, and appeals to bias or prejudice in order to evaluate various forms of historical and contemporary political communication (e.g., Lincoln's "House Divided," Sojourner Truth's "Ain't I a Woman?," Chief Joseph's "I Shall Fight No More Forever," Martin Luther King, Jr.'s "I Have a Dream," campaign advertisements, political cartoons). Standard 19, Grades 9–12 Indicator (McREL, p. 450)

Economics Understands that the evaluation of choices and opportunity costs is subjective and differs across individuals and societies. Standard 1, Grades 6–8 Indicator (McREL, p. 476)

English Language Arts Determines the validity and reliability of primary and secondary source information and uses information accordingly in reporting on a research topic. Standard 4, Grades 9–12 Indicator (McREL, p. 333)

Foreign Language Uses a dictionary or thesaurus written entirely in the target language to select appropriate words for use in preparing written and oral reports. Standard 5, Grades 9–12 Indicator (McREL, p. 506)

Geography Understands the advantages and disadvantages of using maps from different sources and different points of view (e.g., maps developed by the media, business, government, industry, and military to show how a recently closed military installation can be utilized for civilian purposes). Standard 1, Grades 9–12 Indicator (McREL, p. 511)

Health Knows how to determine whether various sources from home, school, and the community present valid health information, products, and services. Standard 1, Grades 9–12 Indicator (McREL, p. 546)

History Knows how to interpret data presented in time lines (e.g., identify the time at which events occurred, the sequence in which events developed, what else was occurring at the time). Historical Understanding Standard 1, Grades 3-5 Indicator (McREL, p. 111)

Life Skills Analyzes arguments to determine if they are supported by facts from books, articles, and databases. Thinking and Reasoning Standard 1, Grades 3-5 Indicator (McREL, p. 607)

Mathematics Knows the difference between pertinent and irrelevant information when solving problems. Standard 1, Grades 3-5 Indicator (McREL, p. 46)

Science Understands how scientific knowledge changes and accumulates over time (e.g., all scientific knowledge is subject to change as new evidence becomes available; some scientific ideas are incomplete and opportunity exists in these areas for new advances; theories are continually tested, revised, and occasionally discarded). Standard 14, Grades 9–12 Indicator (McREL, p. 99)

Standard 3　The student who is information literate uses information accurately and creatively.

The student who is information literate manages information skillfully and effectively in a variety of contexts. That student organizes and integrates information from a range of sources and formats in order to apply it to decision making, problem solving, critical thinking, and creative expression. The student communicates information and ideas for a variety of purposes, both scholarly and creative; to a range of audiences, both in school and beyond; and in print, nonprint, and electronic formats. This Standard promotes the design and execution of authentic products that involve critical and creative thinking and that reflect real world situations. The indicators under this Standard therefore deviate from the traditional definition of use. Rather than suggesting that students simply insert researched information into a perfunctory product, the indicators emphasize the thinking processes involved when students use information to draw conclusions and develop new understandings.

Indicators

Indicator 1. Organizes information for practical application

Levels of Proficiency

Basic Describes several ways to organize information—for example, chronologically, topically, and hierarchically.

Proficient Organizes information in different ways according to the information problem or question at hand.

Exemplary Organizes an information product that presents different types of information in the most effective ways.

Students organize information to make sense of it and to present it most effectively to others. They understand their intended audience, the demands of the presentation format, and the essential ideas in the topic or issue being presented.

Indicator 2. Integrates new information into one's own knowledge

Levels of Proficiency

Basic Recognizes and understands new information and ideas.

Proficient Draws conclusions by combining what is already known about a topic with new information.

Exemplary Integrates one's own previous knowledge with information from a variety of sources to create new meaning.

Students integrate new information into their current knowledge, drawing conclusions by developing new ideas based on information they gather and connecting new ideas with their prior knowledge.

Indicator 3. Applies information in critical thinking and problem solving

Levels of Proficiency

Basic Identifies information that meets a particular information need.

Proficient Uses information from a variety of sources to resolve an information problem or question.

Exemplary Devises creative approaches to using information to resolve information problems or questions.

> Students develop strategies for thinking through and solving information problems by effective synthesizing of appropriate information, new understandings, and conclusions drawn.

Indicator 4. Produces and communicates information and ideas in appropriate formats

Levels of Proficiency

Basic Names a variety of different formats for presenting different kinds of information.

Proficient Chooses an appropriate format for presenting information based on the information itself, the audience, and the nature of the information problem or question.

Exemplary Chooses the most appropriate format for presenting information and justifies that choice.

> Students select the format that most closely matches the needs of their intended audience, the requirements for visual or print representation, and the length of the presentation, and they match the format to the nature and complexity of ideas being presented.

Standards in Action

Grades K–2 (Arts) Throughout the year, students study the culture of various African nations. They design and create papier-mâché masks that highlight various countries and legends from the African continent.

Grades 3-5 (Health) Students create projects for a citywide drug prevention contest. They begin by reflecting on their own concerns about drugs and the effects of drugs in their lives. They gather information from a variety of sources, including speakers' presentations and print, nonprint, and electronic resources. Students choose an appropriate format to communicate their ideas. Students consider posters and other displays, skits, and electronic presentations.

Grades 6–8 (Foreign Language) A French class plans an imaginary trip to Paris. Each student researches information about a particular part of the city to present to the class. Students find historical facts, descriptions of important sites, and information on costs. The class produces a videotape, with the narrative in French, as a travel guide to Paris.

Grades 9–12 (History) High-school seniors predict what their lives will be like in twenty-five years. Working in groups, they identify some broad categories in which rapid change has occurred over the past twenty-five years—e.g., transportation, communication, medicine, manufacturing, and economics. Each group chooses an area and consults reference books to assess the nature and scope of the changes within it. Students use the information as the basis for a class prediction of the changes that will occur in their own lives by their twenty-fifth class reunion.

Examples of Content-Area Standards

Content-area standards that can be linked to information literacy standard 3 include but are not limited to the following examples.

Arts, Theatre Applies research from print and nonprint sources to script writing, acting, design, and directing choices. Standard 5, Grades 5–8 Indicator (McREL, p. 401)

Civics Knows that procedural justice refers to problems arising over fair ways to gather information and make just decisions, and knows examples of situations involving procedural justice (e.g., how should a class president go about deciding which games the class will play). Standard 3, Grades K–2 Indicator (McREL, p. 418)

English Language Arts Synthesizes information from multiple research studies to draw conclusions that go beyond those found in any of the individual studies. Standard 4, Grades 9–12 Indicator (McREL, p. 333)

Foreign Language Presents information about family, school events, and celebrations via letters, e-mail, or in audio- and videotapes. Standard 3, Grades K–4 Indicator (McREL, p. 502)

Geography Transforms primary data into maps, graphs, and charts (e.g., charts developed from recent census data ranking selected information on various topics; cartograms depicting the relative sizes of Latin American countries based on their urban populations). Standard 1, Grades 9–12 Indicator (McREL, p. 511)

Health Knows how to locate and use community health information, products, and services that provide valid health information. Standard 1, Grades 6–8 Indicator (McREL, p. 545)

History Knows how to construct time lines in significant historical developments that mark at evenly spaced intervals the years, decades, or centuries. Historical Understanding Standard 1, Grades 3–5 Indicator (McREL, p. 111)

Life Skills Uses tables, charts, and graphs in constructing arguments. Thinking and Reasoning Standard 1, Grades 9–12 Indicator (McREL, p. 609)

Mathematics Represents problem situations in and translates among oral, written, concrete, pictorial, and graphical forms. Standard 1, Grades 6–8 Indicator (McREL, p. 47)

Physical Education Uses information from fitness assessments to improve selected fitness components (e.g., cardiorespiratory endurance, muscular strength and endurance, flexibility, and body composition). Standard 4, Grades 3–6 Indicator (McREL, p. 569)

Science Designs and conducts scientific investigations by formulating testable hypotheses; identifying and clarifying the question, method, controls, and variables; organizing and displaying data; revising methods and explanations; presenting the results; and receiving critical response from others. Standard 15, Grades 9–12 Indicator (McREL, p. 101)

Technology Knows the common features and uses of desktop publishing software (e.g., documents are created, designed, and formatted for publication; data, graphics, and scanned images can be imported into a document using desktop software). Standard 2, Grades 6–8 Indicator (McREL, p. 581)

INDEPENDENT LEARNING STANDARDS

Standard 4   The student who is an independent learner is information literate and pursues information related to personal interests.

The student who is an independent learner applies the principles of information literacy to access, evaluate, and use information about issues and situations of personal interest. That student actively and independently seeks information to enrich understanding of career, community, health, leisure, and other personal situations. The student constructs meaningful personal knowledge based on that information and communicates that knowledge accurately and creatively across the range of information formats.

Indicators

Indicator 1. Seeks information related to various dimensions of personal well-being, such as career interests, community involvement, health matters, and recreational pursuits

Levels of Proficiency

Basic Occasionally seeks information about aspects of personal interest or well-being.

Proficient Generally goes beyond one's own knowledge to seek information on aspects of personal interest or well-being.

Exemplary Explores a range of sources to find information on aspects of personal interest or well-being.

> Students use the same criteria and strategies to locate and use information on personal topics as they do for academic topics. They test their understanding of information literacy strategies by using them for real-life purposes.

Indicator 2. Designs, develops, and evaluates information products and solutions related to personal interests

Levels of Proficiency

Basic Organizes and presents basic information related to topics of personal interest.

Proficient Creates information products and solutions related to topics of personal interest.

Exemplary Judges the quality of one's own information products and solutions related to topics of personal interest.

Students apply information problem-solving skills to decisions they must make in their personal lives. They share information products with others who are also making personal decisions. They respond to feedback as they reflect on how they can make changes in products and solutions.

Standards in Action

Grades K–2 (Science) It's dinosaur time. Fueled by television shows and by the desire to learn all those long names, students check out dinosaur books and discuss among themselves about which dinosaur was the most ferocious. Some students make stuffed dinosaurs as part of a class project on animals. They seek information on colors, sizes, and shapes of dinosaurs and on places to find dinosaur bones.

Grades 3–5(Foreign Language) Students in a bilingual community idolize a local Hispanic singer. Fascinated with every aspect of this young musician's life, they seek information on her family, schooling, and hobbies as well as on her music. Several friends discuss other resources, such as adult members of the community, the library media center's English- and Spanish-language resources, and Web sites dedicated to the singer.

Grades 6–8 (Mathematics) A student receives a share of computer stock from his grandparents for his birthday. He knows that stocks change in value and wants to keep track of the increases and decreases in the value of the new stock. He decides to get information on the company, to learn to read the daily stock report in the newspaper, and to use a graphing program on the computer to track the progress of the stock.

Grades 9–12 (Health) Students in health classes examine their lifestyles based on health information they have learned. For a week, each student keeps a log of food intake and physical activities. Then, students enter their data into a computer program that evaluates dietary needs based on the standards for the age group and on each individual's level of activity. As a next step, students locate information in magazines, books, and Internet sites to get specific information to build into personal improvement plans based on their health reports.

Examples of Content-Area Standards

Content-area standards that can be linked to information literacy standard 4 include but are not limited to the following examples.

Arts, Dance Improvises, creates, and performs dances based on personal ideas and concepts from other sources. Standard 2, Grades K–4 Indicator (McREL, p. 384)

Civics Knows opportunities for public service in the student's own school, community, state, and nation and knows career opportunities in public service. Standard 29, Grades 6–8 Indicator (McREL, p. 470)

English Language Arts Applies reading skills and strategies to a variety of informational texts (e.g., textbooks, biographical sketches, letters, diaries, directions, procedures, magazines, essays, primary source historical documents, editorials, news stories, periodicals, catalogs, job-related materials, schedules, speeches, memoranda). Standard 7, Grades 9–12 Indicator (McREL, p. 341)

Foreign Language Uses a variety of sources in the target language to obtain information on topics of personal interest. Standard 5, Grades 5–8 Indicator (McREL, p. 505)

Health Knows techniques for seeking help and support through appropriate resources. Standard 2, Grades 3–6 Indicator (McREL, p. 550)

History Understands personal family or cultural heritage through stories, songs, and celebrations. K–4 History Standard 1, Grades K–2 Indicator (McREL, p. 117)

Life Skills Compares consumer products on the basis of features, performance, durability, and cost and considers personal tradeoffs. Thinking and Reasoning Standard 3, Grades 6–8 Indicator (McREL, p. 612)

Physical Education Knows about opportunities for participation in physical activities both in and out of school (e.g., recreational leagues, intramural sports, clubs). Standard 3, Grades 3–6 Indicator (McREL, p. 567)

Science Knows that scientists conduct investigations for a variety of reasons, (e.g., to discover new aspects of the natural world, to explain recently observed phenomena, to test the conclusions of prior investigations, to test the predictions of current theories). Standard 15, Grades 9–12 Indicator (McREL, p. 101)

Technology Connects via modem to other computer users via the internet, an on-line service, or bulletin board system. Standard 1, Grades 6–8 Indicator (McREL, p. 580)

Standard 5   The student who is an independent learner is information literate and appreciates literature and other creative expressions of information.
The student who is an independent learner applies the principles of information literacy to access, evaluate, enjoy, value, and create artistic products. That student actively and independently seeks to master the principles, conventions, and criteria of literature in print, nonprint, and electronic formats. The student is able both to understand and enjoy creative works presented in all formats and to create products that capitalize on each format's particular strengths.

Indicators

Indicator 1. Is a competent and self-motivated reader

Levels of Proficiency
Basic Explains and discusses various examples of fiction.

Proficient Chooses fiction and other kinds of literature to read and analyzes literary plots, themes, and characters.

Exemplary Reads avidly and evaluates the strengths and weaknesses of the literature read.

> Students seek a variety of information resources in different formats for information and personal enjoyment.

Indicator 2. Derives meaning from information presented creatively in a variety of formats

Levels of Proficiency
Basic Explains and discusses films, plays, and other creative presentations of information.

Proficient Analyzes and explains information presented creatively in various formats.

Exemplary Evaluates the strengths and weaknesses of various creative presentations of information.

Students connect to larger ideas in the human experience and their own lives.

Indicator 3. Develops creative products in a variety of formats

Levels of Proficiency

Basic Expresses information and ideas creatively in simple formats.

Proficient Expresses information and ideas creatively in information products that combine several formats.

Exemplary Expresses information and ideas creatively in unique products that integrate information in a variety of formats.

Students can identify and use media that match the purpose of their communication to communicate ideas and emotions most effectively.

Standards in Action

Grades K–2 (Behavioral Studies) Students learn about native peoples of the world. They focus on Indians from North and South America and on African groups. They want to learn all about these groups—their stories, their music, and their art. Students are divided into small groups to design and create group projects that incorporate written, spoken, and visual information.

Grades 3–5 (History) The video *Sarah Plain and Tall* captures the imagination of a fourth-grade girl, who reads the book, its sequel, and other novels about frontier life. She becomes curious about the historical accuracy of the novels and decides to check them against some pioneer women's personal accounts of their lives.

Grades 6–8 (English Language Arts) Sixth-grade language arts students are excited about this year's book discussion program. After listening to a series of book talks, students select seven award-winning books from different genres to read and discuss throughout the year. The discussions—which are led by adults from throughout the school and the community— are informal and open-ended. There are no tests or written assignments.

Grades 9–12 (Arts) Students need information about the lives and times of several visual artists in order to understand how the society of a time influences artists' work. Working in a group structured around a particular geographic area and time period, each student researches one painter, sculptor, and so on from that society. After each group identifies examples of how political, economic, and social factors are reflected in their artists' works, students present a panel on the art of all the societies they have studied.

Examples of Content-Area Standards

Content-area standards that can be linked to information literacy standard 5 include but are not limited to the following examples.

Arts, Theatre Articulates and justifies personal aesthetic criteria for comparing, for dramatic texts and events, perceived artistic intent with the final aesthetic achievement. Standard 5, Grades 9–12 Indicator (McREL, p. 402)

Behavioral Studies Knows that language, stories, folktales, music, and artistic creations are expressions of culture. Standard 2, Grades 3–5 Indicator (McREL, p. 594)

English Language Arts Selects reading material based on personal criteria (e.g., personal interest, knowledge of authors and genres, text difficulty, recommendations of others). Standard 6, Grades 3–5 Indicator (McREL, p. 337)

Foreign Language Understands the main ideas, themes, principal characters, and significant details of ability-appropriate authentic literature. Standard 2, Grades 5–8 Indicator (McREL, p. 501)

Geography Knows how maps help to find patterns of movement in space and time (e.g., mapping hurricane tracks over several seasons, mapping the spread of influenza throughout the world). Standard 1, Grades 6–8 Indicator (McREL, p. 510)

History Understands how stories, legends, songs, ballads, games, and tall tales describe the environment, lifestyles, beliefs, and struggles of people in various regions of the country. K–4 History Standard 6, Grades 3–4 Indicator (McREL, p. 125)

Mathematics Understands that some ways of representing a problem are more helpful than others. Standard 1, Grades 3–5 Indicator (McREL, p. 46)

Science Knows that there is no fixed procedure called "the scientific method" but that investigations involve systematic observations, carefully collected, relevant evidence, logical reasoning, and some imagination in developing hypotheses and explanations. Standard 15, Grades 6–8 Indicator (McREL, p. 100)

Technology Uses desktop publishing software to create a variety of publications. Standard 2, Grades 9–12 Indicator (McREL, p. 582)

Standard 6   The student who is an independent learner is information literate and strives for excellence in information seeking and knowledge generation.

The student who is an independent learner applies the principles of information literacy to evaluate and use his or her own information processes and products as well as those developed by others. That student actively and independently reflects on and critiques personal thought processes and individually created information products. The student recognizes when these efforts are successful and unsuccessful and develops strategies for revising and improving them in light of changing information.

Indicators

Indicator 1. Assesses the quality of the process and products of personal information seeking

Levels of Proficiency

Basic Retraces the steps taken to find information and explains which were most useful for resolving an information problem or question.

Proficient Assesses each step of the information-seeking process related to a specific information problem and assesses the result.

Exemplary Evaluates the information-seeking process at each stage as it occurs and makes adjustments as necessary to improve both the process and the product.

> Students reflect on their own work and revise it based on feedback from others. They develop an intrinsic standard of excellence. They revise their information-searching strategies when appropriate. They also self-assess about their information-seeking process by asking themselves questions such as: Do my questions really get to the heart of what I need to know? and Have I found enough information to give an accurate picture of all sides of the issue? They approach research as a recursive process, revising the search as they answer their own assessment questions. They set their own criteria and check the quality of their own work.

Indicator 2. Devises strategies for revising, improving, and updating self-generated knowledge

Levels of Proficiency

Basic Explains basic strategies for revising, improving, and updating work.

Proficient Selects and applies appropriate strategies for revising, improving, and updating work.

Exemplary Recognizes gaps in one's own knowledge and selects and applies appropriate strategies for filling them.

> Students modify their work based on the specific task, and they use peer review, reaction panels, focus groups, comparison with models, and trial and revision strategies.

Standards in Action

Grades K–2 (Civics) First graders study their community. Each student's final product is a picture of a type of community transportation (truck, bicycle, etc.) and a short report that describes the picture. The teacher shows some of the work of students who have already finished to other students who are still working. One student notices that his picture has only basic elements, while other students have added numerous details. He looks at some picture books about his topic to find some details to add to his picture.

Grades 3–5 (English Language Arts) Students check their final drafts of their reports on Newbery authors before turning them in to the teacher. Although many students had considered their information gathering complete, they now realize that there are holes and gaps in their information. They wonder where to find the additional information they need.

Grades 6–8 (Civics) Two middle-school students work together on a research project on local history. They had assumed their final product would be a traditional written report, and so they gathered printed materials and took extensive notes to prepare to write. Now, they realize that their topic might be better suited to a visual presentation. They consider what other kinds of information sources to use.

Grades 9–12 (Science) The judges award a blue ribbon to a student in the school science fair, and she can now enter the district-level fair. After looking at some of the other projects and papers exhibited at the school fair, she decides she needs more background information to do well at the district level. She thinks that talking to a scientist would provide the most current information, and she decides how to connect with a working scientist.

Examples of Content-Area Standards

Content-area standards that can be linked to information literacy standard 6 include but are not limited to the following examples.

Arts, Visual Arts Understands what makes different art media, techniques, and processes effective (or ineffective) in communicating various ideas. Standard 1, Grades 5–8 Indicator (McREL, p. 404)

Civics Understands how citizens can evaluate information and arguments received from various sources so that they can make reasonable choices on public issues and among candidates for political office. Standard 19, Grades 6–8 Indicator (McREL, p. 449)

English Language Arts Uses strategies to draft and revise written work (e.g., rereads; rearranges words, sentences, and paragraphs to improve or clarify meaning; varies sentence type; adds descriptive words and details; deletes extraneous information; incorporates suggestions from peers and teachers; sharpens the focus). Standard 1, Grades K–2 Indicator (McREL, p. 319)

Health Knows a variety of consumer influences and how those influences affect decisions regarding health resources, products, and services (e.g., media, information from school and family, peer pressure). Standard 1, Grades 3–5 Indicator (McREL, p. 545)

History Knows how to avoid seizing upon particular lessons of history as cures for present ills. Historical Understanding Standard 2, Grades 9–12 Indicator (McREL, p. 114)

Life Skills Reformulates a new hypothesis for study after an old hypothesis has been eliminated. Thinking and Reasoning Standard 4, Grades 6–8 Indicator (McREL, p. 614)

Mathematics Uses a variety of strategies to understand problem-solving situations and processes (e.g., considers different strategies and approaches to a problem, restates problem from various perspectives). Standard 1, Grades 6–8 Indicator (McREL, p. 47)

Physical Education Uses information from a variety of internal and external sources to improve performance (e.g., group projects, student journal, self-assessment, peer and coach review). Standard 2, Grades 3–6 Indicator (McREL, p. 566)

Science Knows that scientific explanations must meet certain criteria to be considered valid (e.g., they must be consistent with experimental and observational evidence about nature, make accurate predictions about systems being studied, be logical, respect the rules of evidence, be open to criticism, report methods and procedures, make a commitment to making knowledge public). Standard 14, Grades 9–12 Indicator (McREL, pp. 98–99)

SOCIAL RESPONSIBILITY STANDARDS

Standard 7 **The student who contributes positively to the learning community and to society is information literate and recognizes the importance of information to a democratic society.**

The student who is socially responsible with regard to information understands that access to information is basic to the functioning of a democracy. That student seeks out information from a diversity of viewpoints, scholarly traditions, and cultural perspectives in an attempt to arrive at a reasoned and informed understanding of issues. The student realizes that equitable access to information from a range of sources and in all formats is a fundamental right in a democracy.

Indicators

Indicator 1. Seeks information from diverse sources, contexts, disciplines, and cultures

Levels of Proficiency

Basic Identifies several appropriate sources for resolving an information problem or question.

Proficient Uses a variety of sources covering diverse perspectives to resolve an information problem or question.

Exemplary Seeks sources representing a variety of contexts, disciplines, and cultures and evaluates their usefulness for resolving an information problem or question.

Students seek diverse opinions and points of view, and they use multiple sources to actively attend to the context surrounding information, such as asking whose opinion, what cultural background, what historical context.

Indicator 2. Respects the principle of equitable access to information

Levels of Proficiency

Basic Explains why it's important for all classmates to have access to information, to information sources, and to information technology.

Proficient Uses information, information sources, and information technology efficiently so that they are available for others to use.

Exemplary Proposes strategies for ensuring that classmates and others have equitable access to information, to information sources, and to information technology.

Students diligently return materials on time, share access to limited resources, are aware of others' rights and needs, and respect equitable access as the dominant culture of learning rather than perceiving it as an environment of strict enforcement of rules.

Standards in Action

Grades K–2 (Civics) Many children in a community are unfamiliar with other cultures. Their school explores the culture of China by hosting a day-long celebration of the Chinese New Year. The day is filled with speakers, crafts, games, entertainment, and foods representing the Chinese culture. Each class uses a variety of resources to plan a "Chinese pavilion" of its own.

Grades 3–5 (Science) Two classes work on reports about marine life. The library media center has adequate information in several formats, but there is only one copy of a series of books on each individual species. The students discuss ways to make sure that everyone can use these resources.

Grades 6–8 (History) Students live in a community that was formed over the years by immigrants from Europe, Africa, and Asia. The class studies local history to determine the influence of each group in creating the present culture. Students find original source materials related to each group's arrival in the community as well as a variety of accounts of the community's earlier days.

Grades 9–12 (English Language Arts) A parent appeals the school's decision to retain *The Catcher in the Rye* as a part of the high-school curriculum. Several students decide to speak in support of the book at the next meeting of the Board of Education. The students realize they need more information on the constitutional right to intellectual freedom in order to prepare their case.

Examples of Content-Area Standards

Content-area standards that can be linked to information literacy standard 7 include but are not limited to the following examples.

Arts, Dance Knows the cultural and historical context of various dances (e.g., colonial America, dances within one's community). Standard 5, Grades K–4 Indicator (McREL, p. 386)

Behavioral Studies Understands how language, literature, the arts, architecture, other artifacts, traditions, beliefs, values, and behaviors contribute to the development and transmission of culture. Standard 2, Grades 6–8 Indicator (McREL, p. 595)

Civics Knows how specific documents in American history set forth shared values, principles, and beliefs (e.g., Declaration of Independence, United States Constitution and Bill of Rights, Pledge of Allegiance). Standard 9, Grades 3–5 Indicator (McREL, pp. 428–429)

English Language Arts Understands influences on language use (e.g., political beliefs, positions of social power, culture). Standard 8, Grades 9–12 Indicator (McREL, p. 345)

Foreign Language Uses verbal and written exchanges to gather and share personal data, information, and opinions (e.g., events in one's life, past experiences, significant details related to topics that are of common interest, opinions about topics of personal or community interest). Standard 1, Grades 5–8 Indicator (McREL, p. 498)

Geography Knows the similarities and differences in characteristics of culture in different regions (e.g., in terms of environment and resources, technology, food, shelter, social organization, beliefs and customs, schooling, what girls and boys are allowed to do). Standard 10, Grades 3–5 Indicator (McREL, p. 524)

History Understands historical figures who believed in the fundamental democratic values (e.g., justice, truth, equality, the rights of the individual, responsibility for the common good, voting rights) and the significance of these people both in their historical context and today. K–4 History Standard 4, Grades 3–4 Indicator (McREL, p. 123)

Science Knows that people of all ages, backgrounds, and groups have made contributions to science and technology throughout history. Standard 16, Grades 3–5 Indicator (McREL, p. 102)

Standard 8 **The student who contributes positively to the learning community and to society is information literate and practices ethical behavior in regard to information and information technology.**

The student who is socially responsible with regard to information applies principles and practices that reflect high ethical standards for accessing, evaluating, and using information. That student recognizes the importance of equitable access to information in a democratic society and respects the principles of intellectual freedom and the rights of producers of intellectual property. The student applies these principles across the range of information formats—print, nonprint, and electronic.

Indicators

Indicator 1. Respects the principles of intellectual freedom

Levels of Proficiency

Basic Defines or gives examples of "intellectual freedom."

Proficient Analyzes a situation (e.g., a challenge to a book or video in the library media center) in terms of its relationship to intellectual freedom.

Exemplary Predicts what might happen if the principles of intellectual freedom were ignored in one's own community.

> Students encourage others to exercise their rights to free expression, they respect the ideas of others when working in groups, and they actively solicit ideas from every member of the group.

Indicator 2. Respects intellectual property rights

Levels of Proficiency

Basic Gives examples of what it means to respect intellectual property rights.

Proficient Analyzes situations (e.g., the creation of a term paper or the development of a multimedia product) to determine the steps necessary to respect intellectual property rights.

Exemplary Avoids plagiarism, cites sources properly, makes copies and incorporates text and images only with appropriate clearance, etc., when creating information products.

Students understand the concept of fair use and apply it, they recognize and diligently avoid plagiarism, they follow an information-seeking process to come to their own conclusions, they express their conclusions in their own words rather than copying the conclusions or arguments presented by others, and they follow bibliographic form and cite all information sources used.

Indicator 3. Uses information technology responsibly

Levels of Proficiency

Basic States the main points of school policy on using computing and communications hardware, software, and networks.

Proficient Locates appropriate information efficiently with the school's computing and communications hardware, software, and networks.

Exemplary Follows all school guidelines related to the use of computing and communications hardware, software, and networks when resolving information problems or questions.

Students follow acceptable use policies and guidelines, using equipment for the purposes intended, and leaving the equipment and materials in good working order.

Standards in Action

Grades K–2 (English Language Arts) Second graders have just learned to use the school's public access catalog (PAC). They are excited about using this new tool to find fiction books in the library media center. A group of students waiting to use the PAC becomes restless as another student keeps looking for more titles, even though she's found five to check out.

Grades 3–5 (Geography) For an assignment about immigration, students write reports on the countries where their own ancestors lived. The students all find sources for their reports, and they understand the information. Students understand that copying word for word from the sources is wrong but are having difficulty putting some of the information in their own words.

Grades 6–8 (Foreign Language) At the beginning of the year, students read and signed the school's computer use policy.

Now a foreign language class is compiling a list of Web sites in Spanish. A group of students unintentionally enters a keyword in Spanish that takes them to a pornographic site. Their "discovery" has now attracted a group of onlookers.

Grades 9–12 (Arts) Students in a film study class create video projects, for which they use original footage in combination with scenes from movies. The projects are so successful that a public-access cable channel wants to run them as part of a film festival. The students must obtain copyright permission for this wider distribution.

Examples of Content-Area Standards

Content-area standards that can be linked to information literacy standard 8 include but are not limited to the following examples.

Arts, Visual Arts Uses art materials and tools in a safe and responsible manner. Standard 1, Grades K–4 Indicator (McREL, p. 404)

Civics Understands contemporary issues that involve economic rights such as consumer product safety, taxation, affirmative action, eminent domain, zoning, copyright, patents. Standard 25, Grades 9–12 Indicator (McREL, p. 462)

English Language Arts Uses a computer catalog to gather information for research topics. Standard 4, Grades 6–8 Indicator (McREL, p. 332)

Geography Understands how communication and transportation technologies contribute to cultural convergence or divergence (e.g., convergence created by electronic media, computers, and jet aircraft; divergence created by technologies used to reinforce nationalistic or ethnic elitism or cultural separateness and independence). Standard 10, Grades 9–12 Indicator (McREL, p. 525)

History Understands the basic principles of American democracy: right to life, liberty, and the pursuit of happiness; responsibility for the common good; equality of opportunity and equal protection of the law; freedom of speech and religion; majority rule with protection for minority rights; and limitations on government, with power held by the people and delegated by them to those officials whom they elected to office. K–4 History Standard 4, Grades 3–4 Indicator (McREL, p. 122)

Mathematics Understands that science and mathematics operate under common principles: belief in order, ideals of honesty and openness, the importance of review by colleagues, and the importance of imagination. Standard 9, Grades 9–12 Indicator (McREL, p. 66)

Science Understands the ethical traditions associated with the scientific enterprise (e.g., commitment to peer review, truthful reporting about methods and outcomes of investigations, publication of the result of work) and that scientists who violate these traditions are censored by their peers. Standard 16, Grades 9–12 Indicator (McREL, p. 103)

Technology Understands the concept of software piracy (i.e., illegally copied software) and that it is a violation of copyright laws. Standard 3, Grades 3–5 Indicator (McREL, p. 583)

Standard 9 The student who contributes positively to the learning community and to society is information literate and participates effectively in groups to pursue and generate information.

The student who is socially responsible with regard to information works successfully—both locally and through the variety of technologies that link the learning community—to access, evaluate, and use information. That student seeks and shares information and ideas across a range of sources and perspectives and acknowledges the insights and contributions of a variety of cultures and disciplines. The student collaborates with diverse individuals to identify information problems, to seek their solutions, and to communicate these solutions accurately and creatively.

Indicators

Indicator 1. Shares knowledge and information with others

Levels of Proficiency
Basic Contributes to group efforts by seeking and communicating specific facts, opinions, and points of view related to information problems or questions.

Proficient Using information sources, selects information and ideas that will contribute directly to the success of group projects.

Exemplary Integrates one's own knowledge and information with that of others in the group.

> Students readily share information they have gathered with others in their group. They discuss ideas with others in the group, listen well, and change their own ideas when appropriate. They also help the group move to consensus after substantive conversation and sharing among all the members of the group.

Indicator 2. Respects others' ideas and backgrounds and acknowledges their contributions

Levels of Proficiency

Basic Describes others' ideas accurately and completely.

Proficient Encourages consideration of ideas and information from all group members.

Exemplary Helps to organize and integrate the contributions of all the members of the group into information products.

> Students actively seek the contributions of every member of the group. They listen well in order to hear the point of view as well as the literal words of what others are saying, and they respond respectfully to the points of view and ideas of others.

Indicator 3. Collaborates with others, both in person and through technologies, to identify information problems and to seek their solutions

Levels of Proficiency

Basic Expresses one's own ideas appropriately and effectively, in person and remotely through technologies, when working in groups to identify and resolve information problems.

Proficient Participates actively in discussions with others, in person and remotely through technologies, to analyze information problems and to suggest solutions.

Exemplary Participates actively in discussions with others, in person and remotely through technologies, to devise solutions to information problems that integrate group members' information and ideas.

Students collaborate with others, both in person and through technologies, to identify information problems and to seek their solutions. They lead, facilitate, negotiate, and otherwise participate in defining the information needs of a group.

Indicator 4. Collaborates with others, both in person and through technologies, to design, develop, and evaluate information products and solutions

Levels of Proficiency
Basic Works with others, in person and remotely through technologies, to create and evaluate simple information products.

Proficient Works with others, in person and remotely through technologies, to create and evaluate products that communicate complex information and ideas.

Exemplary Works with others, in person and remotely through technologies, to create and evaluate complex information products that integrate information in a variety of formats.

Students assume responsibility for collaborating with others, either in person or through technology, to synthesize ideas into a finished product. They initiate reflection and evaluation of their own and the group's work, and they use the evaluation to improve content, delivery, and work habits.

Standards in Action
Grades K–2 (Science) Students work on a project about rain forests and wonder how they will find information. One student mentions that his aunt is an expert on rain forest plants and trees. Another talks about an exhibit on the rain forest he saw at a local aquarium. A third remembers using a CD-ROM about the rain forest at the public library. The students discuss ways they can gather and share all this information.

Grades 3–5 (Geography) A class plays a Web geography game with a class in another country. Time differences have delayed the game on several occasions. Some students are frustrated and want to quit the project. Other students want to continue and research ways to resolve the time problems.

Grades 6–8 (Behavioral Studies) Students work on a project to learn about people with mental and physical disabilities who have made important contributions to society. Through research in reference books, biographies, and periodicals, each student identifies one such person and the skills and strategies that person developed to achieve this success. Students use additional sources to learn more about a particular disability and about the strategies, medications, adaptive equipment, and other mechanisms used by people with that disability.

Grades 9–12 (History) Students work in research groups to investigate the effects of World War II on various countries in Western Europe. Each group finds as much information as possible on a particular country to design a lesson on that country's post-War society and teach its lesson to the rest of the class.

Examples of Content-Area Standards

Content-area standards that can be linked to information literacy standard 9 include but are not limited to the following examples.

Behavioral Studies Knows unique features of different groups to which she or he belongs (e.g., family, team, class) and also features of these groups that overlap with other groups. Standard 2, Grades K–2 Indicator (McREL, p. 593)

Civics Knows some of the benefits of diversity (e.g., it fosters a variety of viewpoints, new ideas, and fresh ways of looking at and solving problems; it provides people with choices in the arts, music, literature, and sports; it helps people appreciate cultural traditions and practices other than their own). Standard 11, Grades 3–5 Indicator (McREL, p. 432)

English Language Arts Evaluates own and others' effectiveness in group discussions and in formal presentations (e.g., evaluates accuracy, relevance, and organization of information; evaluates clarity of delivery; evaluates relationships among purpose, audience, and content; identifies types of arguments used). Standard 8, Grades 9–12 Indicator (McREL, p. 345)

Foreign Language Uses appropriate vocabulary to exchange information about national and international topics (e.g., information from newspaper or magazine articles; programs on television, radio, or video). Standard 1, Grades 9–12 Indicator (McREL, p. 499)

Geography Knows ways that people solve common problems by cooperating (e.g., working in groups to pick up trash along a road, participating in a neighborhood crime-watch group, participating in community house-building projects). Standard 13, Grades K–2 Indicator (McREL, p. 531)

Health Knows how refusal, negotiation, and collaboration skills can be used to avoid potentially harmful situations. Standard 5, Grades 9–12 Indicator (McREL, p. 552)

Life Skills Adjusts tone and content of information to accommodate the likes of others. Working with Others Standard 4, Grades K–12 Indicator (McREL, p. 621)

Science Knows that in science it is helpful to work with a team and share findings with others. Standard 16, Grades K–2 Indicator (McREL, p. 102)

Technology Observes common courtesies and acceptable use policies while telecomputing. Standard 3, Grades 9–12 Indicator (McREL, p. 584)

REFERENCES

Bloom, Benjamin S., Max D. Englehart, Edward J. Furst, Walker H. Hill, and David R. Krathwohl. *A Taxonomy of Educational Objectives: Handbook I. The Cognitive Domain.* New York: David McKay, 1956.
   Outlines levels of learning.
California School Library Association. *From Library Skills to Information Literacy: A Handbook for the 21st Century.* Castle Rock, Colo.: Hi Willow, 1997.
   Provides a framework for an information literacy curriculum as well as recommendations for student assessment.
Craver, Kathleen W. *Teaching Electronic Literacy: A Concepts-Based Approach for School Library Media Specialists.* Westport, Conn.: Greenwood Press, 1997.
   Identifies the concepts that students must learn in order to be information literate in an electronic environment. Sample lesson plans provide effective models for how concepts can be taught.

Eisenberg, Mike, and Bob Berkowitz. *The Big 6 Newsletter: Teaching Technology and Information Skills.* Worthington, Ohio: Linworth Publishing.

Published six times per year with practical advice and ideas for teaching information literacy and real-life experiences from the field.

Fitzgerald, Mary Ann. "Misinformation on the Internet: Applying Evaluation Skills to Online Information." *Emergency Librarian* (January–February 1997): 9–14.

Suggests what must be taught as students confront information on the Internet and must evaluate information in an unjuried environment.

Jansen, Barbara. "Reading for Information: The Trash-N-Treasure Method of Teaching Notetaking." *School Library Media Activities Monthly* (February 1996): 29–32.

Provides a practical technique for teaching notetaking.

Kendall, John S. and Robert J. Marzano. *Content Knowledge: A Compendium of Standards and Benchmarks for K–12 Education.* 2nd ed. Denver, Colo.: Midcontinent Research and Evaluation Laboratory, 1997.

Contains content-area standards written by national standards writing groups.

Kuhlthau, Carol. "Implementing a Process Approach to Information Skills: A Study Identifying Indicators of Success in Library Media Programs." *School Library Media Quarterly* (Fall 1993): 11–18.

Reviews the information search process and identifies aspects of the program that lead to successful implementation of an information literacy program.

McElmeel, Sharron L. *Research Strategies for Moving beyond Reporting.* Worthington, Ohio: Linworth Publishing, 1997.

Offers a practical guide and rationale to help students learn the research process by doing primary research. Provides diverse strategies and formats for students to communicate what they have learned.

McKenzie, Jamie. "A Questioning Toolkit." *From Now On: The Educational Technology Journal* 7, no. 3 (November/December 1997). Online: <http://www.fromnowon.org/>

Based on the idea that research begins with a question but students may have difficulty with this step, explores seventeen types of questions and how students can use them.

Stripling, Barbara K. "Quality in School Library Media Programs: Focus on Learning." *Library Trends* 14, no. 3 (Winter 1996): 631–656.

Surveys instruction in school library media centers from its early focus on source location and retrieval to its current emphasis on an information search process approach. Comments on the school library media specialist roles of change agent and catalyst for curriculum reform.

PART TWO

BUILDING PARTNERSHIPS
FOR LEARNING

Chapter 3

Collaboration, Leadership, and Technology

Students today live in a challenging, exciting world of information within a society that is increasingly dependent on knowledge. A dynamic, student-centered library media program fosters information literacy and lifelong learning—the basis for true information power. The school library media specialist's opportunities for cultivating authentic, information-based learning have never been greater, and the responsibilities are also more crucial than ever before.

A clear and creative vision is essential in guiding a strong and vibrant program that allows the school library media specialist to serve the learning community of students and others in a rapidly changing information world. Such a vision also allows the library media specialist to enjoy the unprecedented rewards that come from working with a learning community engaged in active, creative thinking and problem solving.

Three basic ideas—collaboration, leadership, and technology—underlie the vision of library media programs presented in *Information Power: Building Partnerships for Learning*. These ideas provide unifying themes for guiding the effective library media specialist and for infusing all the activities, services, and functions of an effective, student-centered program.

As with the standards, the unifying ideas are discussed here as broad concepts. School library media specialists must determine how to interpret these themes and incorporate them into the functions of their individual school media programs. The dynamics of each situation—local policies, personnel, budgets, and communities—and the individual school library media specialist's own style are factors to be considered. Obstacles may also be encountered: some school administrators may be resistant to strong leadership; some budgets will preclude expansion of technology use; and some teachers may not take advantage of the school library media specialist's collaborative efforts. These situations and others like them require creative efforts by school library media specialists to actualize collaboration, leadership, and technology in the school library media program.

INFORMATION POWER—THE BIGGER PICTURE

To understand the importance of collaborating, leading, and using technology in building a learning community, we need to describe these themes within the larger context of creating learning-centered library media centers. The *Information Power* logo visually represents the components that sustain a powerful vision for the twenty-first century.

The ultimate goal behind this vision is to help students become full members of the **learning community**—the global web of individuals and organizations who are interconnected in a lifelong quest

The *Information Power* Logo

to understand and meet constantly changing information needs. Library media programs are vital neighborhoods for the learning community, and library media specialists are crucial to their neighborhoods' success. By exerting leadership as they work in collaboration with teachers, administrators, and others to use information technology to help learners meet their information needs, library media specialists bring the learning community to life.

Collaboration, leadership, and **technology** are integral to every aspect of the library media program and every component of the library media specialist's role. They furnish theoretical and practical grounding both for the program and for all the activities of the library media specialist; which include serving as an instructional partner in learning and teaching, providing information access and delivery, and administering and managing the program. They suggest a framework that surrounds and supports the authentic student learning that is the goal of a successful, student-centered library media program.

The three intersecting circles within the logo—**learning and teaching**, **information access**, and **program administration**—are the essential elements of school library media programs. These elements suggest the roles that the library media specialist plays in supporting student learning. The functions and services necessary to the learning and teaching and the information access roles will promote that learning directly; program administration activities offer underlying organizational support to the program.

At the center of the *Information Power* logo is **student learning**. Nurturing authentic student learning within and beyond the curriculum is at the core of an effective library media program. Educators have come to recognize that the concepts and skills of information literacy are basic components of lifelong, independent learning. By helping students master information literacy—which is essential to mastering curricular content, critical thinking, and problem solving—the library media program makes a unique and indispensable contribution to their learning.

The information literacy standards for student learning are a tool for supporting and structuring students' development as lifelong, independent learners. This tool—which presents learning outcomes for students from the elementary grades through high school—is designed to help library media specialists infuse information literacy throughout the content areas of the curriculum. As the primary vehicle for linking library media programs and library media specialists with learning, the information literacy standards are the key to implementing the vision that underlies *Information Power: Building Partnerships for Learning.*

COLLABORATION

Collaboration—working with others—is a key theme in building partnerships for learning. Library media specialists have long understood the importance of collaborating with the different members of the learning community. The literature of the field, both from research and from practice, documents the importance of collaborative planning and teaching and describes imaginative and successful collaborative efforts.

Today, as the library media specialist's role becomes even more closely linked with the curriculum, the significance of collaboration throughout the learning process is increasingly important. Collaboration is essential as library media specialists work with teachers to plan, conduct, and evaluate learning activities that incorporate information literacy. It is critical as they work with teachers and administrators to build and manage collections that include all formats and that support authentic, information-based learning.

Source: Photograph courtesy of Oregon Educational Media Associaton.

And it is basic as they work with teachers, administrators, parents, and other members of the learning community to plan, design, and implement programs that provide access to the information that is required to meet students' and others' learning goals.

As the catalyst for collaboration, the library media specialist initiates collaborative efforts that are focused on meeting the learning needs of students, both within and beyond the library media center. Working to establish links not only between the library media program and individual teachers but among the teachers themselves, the library media specialist encourages a culture of collaboration throughout the school. Effective collaboration with teachers helps to create a vibrant and engaged community of learners, strengthens the whole school program as well as the library media program, and develops support for the school library media program throughout the whole school.

PRACTICAL APPROACHES TO COLLABORATING

- Establish a good relationship with teachers; be approachable
- Raise teachers' expectations of what the school library media program can do
- Become an expert on the curriculum's goals
- Show the connections between information literacy and content-related objectives
- Solicit teachers' assistance in library media program development
- Be flexible in expectations and timing
- Be persistent

Source: Adapted from Linda Wolcott, "Planning with Teachers: Practical Approaches to Collaboration." *Emergency Librarian* (January–February 1996): 9–14.

Collaboration is a symbiotic process that requires active, genuine effort and commitment by all members of the instructional team. It may take considerable time and energy to establish truly collaborative relationships, but developing effective collaboration strategies is crucial to the library media program. Collaborating with the full range of school personnel to identify and solve information problems presents a model of the approach that students and others must take to thrive in the information age.

LEADERSHIP

Steady and visionary leadership is widely evident in effective school library media programs. Although leadership strategies often work subtly behind the scenes, the information society offers library media specialists many new opportunities to use more visible leadership strategies. For example, exerting strong curricular and instructional leadership helps the library media specialist clarify the nature of learning in an information-rich environment and promote a curriculum in which information literacy provides a coherent thread across all subjects and grade levels. Similarly, the library media specialist takes the lead in educational reform by showing the connections between information-based learning and the skills students will need in the twenty-first century. The school library media specialist takes a proactive role in promoting the use of technology by staff, in determining staff development needs, in facilitating staff learning explorations, and by serving as a leader in staff

Source: American Library Association photo by Leslie Slavin. Courtesy of the National Library Power Program.

development activities. The library media specialist can be a leading advocate for information literacy as a basic component of authentic, independent learning.

Leadership for the library media specialist involves "leading from the middle" as well as assuming more visible, proactive leadership roles. This type of leadership includes coaching others to do for themselves, acting as a sounding board for key decision-makers, bringing people together, and taking the risk of leading when the opportunity arises (Herrin, 1993). By fostering information literacy and authentic learning among students and others, the library media specialist encourages members of the learning community to acquire knowledge and skills that will enhance their own contributions to school and society. The library media specialist can also lead on another level by fostering collaboration and building effective teams throughout the school and the broader community and by encouraging informed opinions. Pursuing opportunities for staff development and continuing education also allows the library media specialist to model and promote lifelong learning by example.

School leaders also need courage. On the practical side, they need to set an example by using whatever tools are built into the school for their own work, such as e-mail, word processing, and so on. But school leaders also need to be able to help teachers through the process of articulating the connection between technology and their instructional goals—and broader school reform goals.

Source: Barbara Means, quoted in Anne Turnbaugh Lockwood, "Views from Research and Practice: Technology's Transformation of Teaching and Learning," *New Leaders for Tomorrow's Schools* 5, no. 1 (Winter 1998).

The library media specialist exercises leadership in both formal and informal ways. The library media specialist helps learners understand and achieve information literacy and the authentic learning it supports. In less obvious ways—for example, by showing enthusiasm for the value of contribution, by nurturing students to become full members of the learning community, and by recruiting talented newcomers to the library media profession and mentoring them as they work to achieve their potential—the school library media specialist also shows effective leadership strategies.

TECHNOLOGY

Along with collaboration and leadership, technology is an important aspect of the school library media program. The earliest modern information technologies—whether the card catalog or the microfiche—brought library media specialists to the forefront of technology use to enhance information access and use. Today's electronic information technologies have transformed society and the library media specialist's role as well. The nature, quantity, and availability of information today and the rapid evolution of information technologies have helped to breed a need for continuous learning. Members of the learning community can access information more efficiently and more effectively than ever before. They look to new, personally rewarding and socially responsible methods to evaluate and use that information.

"Instructional technology is the theory and practice of design, development, utilization, management, and evaluation of processes and resources for learning."—Barbara B. Seels and Rita C. Richey, *Instructional Technology: The Definition and Domains of the Field.* (Washington, D.C.: Association for Educational Communications and Technology, 1994).

The focus of this definition is on technology as a process rather than as only a product. The use of technological processes and resources to enhance learning rather than only to manipulate data supports the library media specialist's use of the full range of techniques and technologies to promote learning.

The library media specialist is a primary leader in the school's use of all kinds of technologies—both instructional and informational—to enhance learning. Acting as a technologist (rather than a technician) and a collaborator with teachers, the library media specialist plays a critical role in designing student experiences that focus on authentic learning, information literacy, and curricular mastery—not simply on manipulating machinery. A technician works with hardware and systems software, while the school library media specialist uses technology from the perspective of the technologist, integrating people, learning, and the tools of technology. Using the technologist's concepts and tools, the school library media specialist analyzes a need, designs a way to meet it, tests the design, and

Source: Courtesy of *Brainerd Daily Dispatch.*

evaluates and revises it. By being knowledgeable about both the structure and presentation of information and about the operation of the devices that deliver that information, the library media specialist brings a broad expertise to teachers' and administrators' discussions of technological issues. The library media specialist draws upon that unique expertise to play a leading role in collaborating with the learning community to plan, design, implement, and continually refine an effective, student-centered technology plan. Such a plan focuses on helping students and others become independent, lifelong learners who use information and information technology profitably, responsibly, and ethically.

These three themes—collaboration, leadership, and technology—are interwoven throughout *Information Power: Building Partnerships for Learning.* They offer a rich image of the contribution that an energetic and vital program brings to the learning community. They suggest the basic assumptions on which this document rests and with which the library media specialist can forge a successful, visionary library media program for the dawn of the twenty-first century.

REFERENCES

Collaboration

Berkowitz, Robert E. et al. "Collaboration: Partnerships for Instructional Improvement." *School Library Media Activities Monthly* 10, no. 7 (March 1994): 32–35.

   Addresses two critical questions related to integrating information literacy into the curriculum: 1) how to select the best opportunities within the content curriculum with which to integrate and 2) how to design instructional units that motivate students to learn and use information problem-solving skills effectively.

Donham van Deusen, Jean. "The School Library Media Specialist as a Member of the Teaching Team: Insider and Outsider." *Journal of Curriculum and Supervision* 11, no. 3 (Spring 1996): 229–248.

   Describes a case study in which the library media specialist plays distinctive roles as a member of each teaching team in an elementary school. Team roles are identified and the library media specialist's impact on teaching and learning is described.

Putnam, Eleonor. "The Instructional Consultant Role of the Elementary School Library Media Specialist and the Effects of Program Scheduling on Its Practice." *School Library Media Quarterly* 25, no. 1 (Fall 1996): 43–49.

   Reports a study of 296 American Library Association members that found that although library media specialists support the instructional consultant role as stated in *Information Power,* they lagged in its practice; notes that library media specialists who used flexible scheduling practiced the instructional consultant role more than those who used fixed scheduling.

Wolcott, Linda. "Planning with Teachers: Practical Approaches to Collaboration." *Emergency Librarian* (January–February 1996): 9–14.

   Describes the practical aspects of working with teachers by describing how teachers plan and then how the library media specialist can effectively collaborate in that process.

Leadership

Donham, Jean. *Enhancing Teaching and Learning: A Leadership Guide for School Library Media Specialists.* New York: Neal Schuman, 1997.

   Identifies the ways in which the library media program interacts with all segments of the learning community to improve teaching and learning.

Farmer, Lesley S. J. *Workshops for Teachers: Becoming Partners for Information Literacy.* Worthington, Ohio: Linworth Publishing, 1995.

   Provides rationale for collaboration between library media specialists and classroom teachers in the teaching of information literacy. Also offers practical guidelines and ideas for implementing staff development activities in the collaboration process.

Hartzell, Gary N. *Building Influence for the School Librarian.* Worthington, Ohio: Linworth Publishing, 1994.

   A former principal and district administrator looks at advocacy from the standpoint of benefits to stakeholders, emphasizes the importance of shaping the perceptions of others, and provides strategies for building a power base in the school.

Herrin, Barbara. "Leading from the Middle." *Library Power* 1, no. 3 (Fall 1993): 3.
    Develops ideas for a unique leadership style for school library media specialists.

Loertscher, David V. *Reinvent Your School's Library in the Age of Technology: A Guide for Principals and Superintendents.* Castle Rock, Colo.: Hi Willow Research & Publishing, 1998.
    Highlights the role of the library media center in collaboration, reading, enhancing learning through technology, information literacy, and building the information infrastructure. Includes checklists, plans, methods of evaluation, budgeting practices.

Technology

Baule, Steven M. *Technology Planning.* Worthington, Ohio: Linworth Publishing, 1997.
    Offers a comprehensive approach to technology integration into the curriculum including many practical ideas based on real-life experiences.

Bialo, Ellen R., and Jay Sivin-Kachala. "The Effectiveness of Technology in Schools: A Summary of Recent Research." *School Library Media Quarterly* 25, no. 1 (Fall 1996): 51–57.
    Summarizes educational technology research conducted from 1990 through 1995. Looks at effects of technology on learning, on students' self-concepts and attitudes about learning, and on interactions involving teachers and students in the learning environment.

Kuhlthau, Carol, ed. *The Virtual School Library: Gateway to the Information Superhighway.* Englewood, Colo.: Libraries Unlimited, 1996.
    Essays deal with issues facing library media specialists who are wrestling with the changes brought on by technology in the schools. Topics range from thinking skills to information curriculum and distance education. The original articles appeared in School Library Media Annual.

Lamb, Annette, and Larry Johnson. *Strap on Your Spurs: Technology and Change Cowboy Style.* Emporia, Kansas: Vision to Action Publishing, 1994.
    Contains strategies for designing, developing, implementing, and evaluating school technology programs.

Talab, Rosemary. "Copyright, Legal and Ethical Issues in the Internet Environment." *Tech Trends* 39, no. 2 (March 1994): 11–14.
    Interprets the copyright laws related to a wide range of information issues connected with access through the Internet.

Wiburg, Karin. "Becoming Critical Users of Multimedia." *The Computing Teacher* 22, no. 7 (Apr. 1995): 59–61.
    Summarizes various studies investigating the effectiveness of technology in learning and teaching situations; emphasizes the potential of technology for encouraging creative and critical thinking. Underscores the importance of multimedia software that supports thoughtful interaction among learners and provides for different learning styles.

Chapter 4

Learning and Teaching

LEARNING AND TEACHING PRINCIPLES OF SCHOOL LIBRARY MEDIA PROGRAMS

Principle 1: The library media program is essential to learning and teaching and must be fully integrated into the curriculum to promote students' achievement of learning goals.

Principle 2: The information literacy standards for student learning are integral to the content and objectives of the school's curriculum.

Principle 3: The library media program models and promotes collaborative planning and curriculum development.

Principle 4: The library media program models and promotes creative, effective, and collaborative teaching.

Principle 5: Access to the full range of information resources and services through the library media program is fundamental to learning.

Principle 6: The library media program encourages and engages students in reading, viewing, and listening for understanding and enjoyment.

Principle 7: The library media program supports the learning of all students and other members of the learning community who have diverse learning abilities, styles, and needs.

Principle 8: The library media program fosters individual and collaborative inquiry.

Principle 9: The library media program integrates the uses of technology for learning and teaching.

Principle 10: The library media program is an essential link to the larger learning community.

These principles were identified and developed by the Information Power Vision Committee, reviewed and commented upon by the profession, and approved by the AASL and AECT Boards as the cardinal premises on which learning and teaching within the effective school library media program is based.

LEARNING AND TEACHING WITHIN THE SCHOOL LIBRARY MEDIA PROGRAM

The primary goal of any school is learning. As effective teaching and learning theory has shifted from a teacher-centered to a student-centered perspective, the school library media program has adapted and has become more important than ever in achieving the school's goal. The quality of library media programs is inextricably linked to the quality of education offered in the schools. Schools have evolved to focus on learning, and effective school library media programs have also changed their focus from collections to learning that engages students in pursuing knowledge within and beyond a formal curriculum.

Schools must identify the behaviors of problem solving and thinking—or human competence—as they appear in authentic settings and then attempt to create academic experiences that develop the kinds of skills and strategies that characterize successful intellectual work. Three dimensions characterize such work:

- *Construction of knowledge* calls for students to engage in higher order thinking skills to arrive at conclusions that produce new meaning or understanding for them; this contrasts with reproducing information provided to them.
- *Disciplined inquiry* calls for deep knowledge where students explore interconnections and relationships rather than fragmented pieces of information. In disciplined inquiry, students pose questions and seek information not to become literate on a topic but to solve a problem or resolve an issue.
- *Connections beyond school* means that the work students do should have value beyond being an indicator of success in school—either a real world public problem, personal experience, or communication beyond the school to inform or influence.

Source: Fred Newmann, Walter Secada, and Gary Wehlage, *A Guide to Authentic Instruction and Assessment: Vision, Standards, and Scoring* (Madison, Wisc.: Wisconsin Center for Education Research, 1995).

A professional school library media specialist is essential to create a dynamic program that challenges students to create personal meaning from information and to participate in a collaborative culture of learning.

An effective school library media program is based on the best research and practice in the field.

- It demonstrates how collaborative teaching that stresses information literacy supports active, authentic learning throughout the school.
- It engages students in learning to help them grow into lifelong learners who pursue knowledge within and beyond a formal curriculum.
- It models a vibrant, collaborative culture of learning and promotes full participation by the entire learning community.

The school library media specialist can provide strong and creative leadership in building and nurturing this culture of learning, both as a teacher and as an instructional partner. As a teacher, the school library media specialist uses both traditional materials and innovative resources, such as electronic media, to help the learning community become information literate. As an instructional partner, the school library media specialist offers a unique expertise in learning theory, information literacy, and information technology to promote learning.

This chapter focuses on how the library media specialist can use the information literacy standards for student learning to address learning and teaching aspects of the library media program. The content is written from a broad perspective to encourage local adaptation of the concepts. The themes underlying *Information Power*—collaboration, leadership, and technology—are interwoven throughout the chapter.

Principle 1   The library media program is essential to learning and teaching and must be fully integrated into the curriculum to promote students' achievement of learning goals.

To promote students' achievement of learning goals, connections between content learning and information skills must be interwoven into every level of student learning. Students need many carefully planned opportunities to access, use, and evaluate information in all subject areas and in all formats. With its grounding in the concepts and processes of information literacy, the school library media program helps students and others within the learning community become information literate as they achieve their content learning goals.

To promote the full integration of information literacy and content learning, the school library media specialist also participates on curriculum and technology committees throughout the school. As an educational leader and as an equal partner of the instructional staff, the library media specialist collaborates in curriculum development and technology planning at all levels to promote information literacy's central place in the curriculum. The library media specialist is also an advocate for information-literacy goals and objectives at the state, district, and building levels and in all subject areas and grade levels. These steps will help ensure that information literacy is an integral part of every student's learning experience.

Goals for the School Library Media Specialist

1. Develop a thorough knowledge of subject area and grade level curricula, and promote competency in information literacy across the curriculum

2. Work on subject area and grade level teams and committees at the building, district, and state levels
   - to develop curriculum
   - to establish learning goals and objectives that incorporate information literacy skills
   - to recommend appropriate information resources to support information literacy and critical thinking throughout the curriculum

3. Participate on technology committees at all levels to focus technology plans on information literacy

4. Collaborate with teachers, staff, and other members of the learning community to integrate information literacy competencies throughout the teaching and learning process

Principle 2   The information literacy standards for student learning are integral to the content and objectives of the school's curriculum.

The information literacy standards for student learning are the foundation for the school library media program. They provide intellectual integration of information skills, including communication, analysis, synthesis, organization, and evaluation skills. They demonstrate clearly that information skills are integral to learning and teaching and should be linked to the curriculum in every subject

Source: American Library Association photo by Leslie Slavin. Courtesy of the National Library Power Program.

area and grade level. By showing how information literacy fosters critical thinking and problem solving in all disciplines and for students at all levels, the standards create a strong theoretical base for the library media program's central role in the culture of learning.

The standards also form the basis for the library media specialist's collaborative efforts to infuse the services and resources of the program throughout the curriculum. They can be used to structure student learning within the library media program and to build and maintain teaching-and-learning partnerships throughout the school, as they illustrate how information literacy underlies students' achievement in all content areas. They also support the library media specialist as a strong advocate for integrated, information-based instruction that helps students become active and independent learners.

Goals for the School Library Media Specialist

1. Develop a deep understanding of the information literacy standards for student learning and of the specific relationships

between the standards and the curricular goals of the school and the district

2. Create and promote a rationale for infusing the information literacy standards for student learning into curricular and instructional policies for the district and the school

3. Develop and promote specific plans for incorporating the information literacy standards for student learning into day-to-day curricular and instructional activities

4. Collaborate regularly with teachers and other members of the learning community to encourage students to become information literate, independent in their learning, and socially responsible in their use of information and information technology

Principle 3   The library media program models and promotes collaborative planning and curriculum development.
Research and practice have established the school library media program's vital role in collaborative planning and curriculum development. Serving all grade levels, ages, and content areas, the program has a unique outlook on the needs and abilities of all the members of the school's learning community. That perspective makes the school library media program a natural hub for bringing teachers and library media specialists together to create exemplary and innovative curricula. The program also offers a model for weaving content-area goals and information literacy skills into active, authentic learning experiences. The effective program's activities and services use collaborative planning and curriculum development to support strong instructional partnerships that lead to students' development of essential critical-thinking and problem-solving skills.

The information literacy standards for student learning provide the basis for the library media specialist's role in collaborative planning and curriculum development. By showing specific links between information literacy and the content area standards adopted by various national groups, the standards offer a concrete starting place for designing integrated instruction and for collaborative planning, teaching, and evaluation. They strongly support the school library media specialist's leadership role in analyzing learning needs, identifying instructional strategies and resources, and evaluating student achievement.

Goals for the School Library Media Specialist

1. Use the information literacy standards for student learning as a basis for curricular and instructional planning

2. Collaborate regularly with teachers and other members of the learning community to develop curricular content that integrates information-literacy skills, to plan instructional activities, and to identify resources that support and enhance the curriculum

3. Teach and assess student achievement of information-literacy concepts and processes as determined through collaborative planning with teachers and other members of the learning community

Principle 4   The library media program models and promotes creative, effective, and collaborative teaching.
The library media program provides a central resource for successful and imaginative teaching. Its collection includes current, authoritative materials on learning and instructional theories, and its activities promote collaborative and innovative approaches to developing the concepts and skills needed in the information age. Through both formal and informal means, the school library media program exemplifies instructional ideas and patterns that promote the active construction of knowledge. The program demonstrates that information literacy—the ability to access, use, and evaluate information in all sources and formats—is a key ingredient in the mastery of subject-matter outcomes.

For students and other members of the learning community, the library media specialist provides leadership and direction in creating and presenting activities and resources that enhance learning. Individually and in collaboration with other faculty, the library media specialist applies the principles of instructional design to develop, implement, evaluate, and revise instruction that meets students' learning needs, including strategies for assessment of student performance in information literacy. The library media specialist, skilled in integrating subject-matter instruction and the concepts and skills of information literacy, creates learning experiences that engage students in the active construction of personal knowledge through the use of a wide variety of information sources and formats. Collaboration may involve teachers and library media specialists working together throughout the planning and implementation process, or it may necessitate the division of responsibilities once learning goals and basic strategies have been identified.

Goals for the School Library Media Specialist

1. Maintain a current professional collection that supports instructional excellence across the curriculum

2. Design and implement teaching and learning activities, both individually and in collaboration with other faculty, that reflect the best in current research and practice

3. Apply basic principles of instructional design in creating activities and resources for learning

4. Promote the full range of information literacy skills in such areas as reading programs, literature appreciation, information-seeking skills, and the uses of information technology

5. Promote information literacy skills to teachers and other staff as integral to subject-matter learning in all areas

Principle 5   Access to the full range of information resources and services through the library media program is fundamental to learning.
The school library media program is grounded in the belief that access to information in all formats, at all levels, and to all members of the learning community is a crucial component of a culture of learning. The effective program offers a wide array of materials and services to help meet learning needs both within and beyond school walls. It can be the gateway to all the information resources the learning community needs for active, constructive learning.

As the school's expert in information issues, the school library media specialist can play a central role in evaluating, acquiring, providing, and promoting information resources both within and beyond the library media center. The library media specialist is the school's authority on accessing, evaluating, and using information in all formats—teachers, administrators, and others rely on the library media specialist's guidance in these areas. Collaboration with the faculty and staff is essential to the successful integration of information resources to achieve learning goals.

Goals for the School Library Media Specialist

1. Build and maintain expertise in a wide range of information issues, resources, and technology

2. Collaborate with teachers, administrators, and others to ensure that the full range of information resources is available to promote student learning

3. Evaluate, acquire, provide, and promote information resources to meet the learning needs of all learners

4. Advise and assist the school community in evaluating and acquiring school-based information resources

5. Establish and maintain ties with information resources and services within the local community that can help meet learning needs

6. Participate in electronic networks and resource sharing systems that expand the library media center's capacity to access information globally

Principle 6   The library media program encourages and engages students in reading, viewing, and listening for understanding and enjoyment.
Library media programs are justly proud of their long tradition of providing reading, listening and viewing guidance to students and others in the learning community. Strong and imaginative activities that promote reading have always been a staple of program offerings, and over the years the program's focus has expanded to promote critical viewing and listening skills as well. These core abilities of reading, viewing, and listening, along with writing and communication, form the basis for developing information literacy skills that are equally basic for today's students. Through its promotion of the pleasure and fulfillment to be derived from using various media for both information and recreation, the library media program educates and encourages the school community in the uses of all communication tools.

The school library media specialist is ideally situated to work collaboratively and in a leadership role with classroom teachers, reading specialists, film/video and media teachers, technology specialists, and others to illustrate the link between successful living and effective skills in reading, listening, and viewing.

Source: American Library Association photo by Leslie Slavin. Courtesy of the
National Library Power Program.

Goals for the School Library Media Specialist

1. Model the effective and enthusiastic use of books, videos, films, multimedia, and other creative expressions of information as sources of pleasure and information

2. Work collaboratively and individually to design, develop, and implement programs that encourage reading for enjoyment and for information

3. Work collaboratively and individually to design, develop, and implement programs that develop skills in media literacy, including the critical analysis of film, television, and other mass media

4. Become an advocate inside and outside the school for reading and for literacy in print, graphic, and electronic formats

Principle 7 The library media program supports the learning of all students and other members of the learning community who have diverse learning abilities, styles, and needs.

The school library media program must meet the learning needs of all the members of a school's learning community—students, teachers, parents, administrators, and the local community. Cognitive theory highlights individuality in learning, and the library media program provides a wide range of materials, activities, and services to address the full range of individuals' learning abilities, styles, and needs. Various developmental levels, physical and intellectual disabilities, special gifts and talents, diverse cultural backgrounds, and different styles of accessing and processing information are supported by the collection and functions of the library media program.

Collaboration with the other members of the learning community is essential to ensure that the school library media program is able to meet individual learning needs of students. The school library media specialist takes the lead in identifying students' information needs; in developing strategies that will help students access, evaluate, and use information from a variety of sources; in providing appropriate and effective resources and instruction; and in evaluating students' needs, interests, and achievements.

Goals for the School Library Media Specialist

1. Maintain a collection that is diverse in format and content to support the learning needs of students and other members of the learning community with a wide spectrum of abilities, backgrounds, needs, and learning styles

2. Work individually and collaboratively with other faculty to analyze individual students' learning needs, particularly as they relate to information literacy

3. Recommend appropriate resources and activities to meet individuals' learning needs

4. Apply basic principles of instructional design to develop learning activities

5. Create, implement, and evaluate resources in various formats to meet individuals' learning needs, and assess students' achievement

6. Develop activities and resources to address the individual needs of all members of the learning community, particularly students, in mastering the concepts of information literacy and the uses of information resources and technology

Principle 8   The library media program fosters individual and collaborative inquiry.

Inquiry is an essential component of learning in the information age, and the library media program is the keystone in a school's efforts to promote efficient and effective self-directed inquiry. The library media program furnishes physical access to the full range of information resources needed by the learning community. The program also provides intellectual access to these resources to enable both individuals and groups to solve their information problems, to satisfy their curiosity, and to construct personal meaning through the research process. Grounded in the concepts and techniques of information literacy, the program is a primary venue for students and others to develop expertise in inquiry—that is, in gathering, understanding, and communicating information.

The school library media specialist is a catalyst in generating a spirit of inquiry within the learning community. By modeling the processes of successful inquiry, the school library media specialist also takes the lead in promoting the habits and skills of lifelong, self-directed learning. By collaborating with teachers and others to help students develop successful information-seeking strategies, the library media specialist demonstrates the value of working in groups to solve information problems. And by promoting careful and precise work at every stage of inquiry, the library media specialist underscores responsible information seeking and use.

Goals for the School Library Media Specialist

1. Provide students and other members of the learning community with intellectual access to the full range of information resources, both traditional and electronic, as appropriate to their learning needs

2. Model the attitudes and skills of an independent, lifelong learner who values inquiry and is competent in all its stages and with all its tools

3. Collaborate with teachers and others to educate students in the steps and criteria for efficient and effective inquiry

4. Promote excellence and responsibility in individual and group uses of information and information technology

5. Promote the information literacy standards for student learning as guidelines for student engagement with the full array of information resources.

Principle 9   The library media program integrates the uses of technology for learning and teaching.
The school library media center is the natural home for the various technologies that serve the learning community. Technology as a *product* is readily apparent in the program's collection of instructional and informational resources like videos and CD-ROMs; technology as a *process* for solving learning problems is embodied in the program's commitment to the concepts and skills of instructional design. Today's explosion of electronic information resources offers a singular opportunity for the library media program to combine the products and processes of technology to create and support unprecedented teaching and learning experiences. The information literacy standards for student learning are a comprehensive framework for designing and implementing the information-based activities that are the core of authentic learning.

As one of the school's experts in information technology processes and products, in instructional and learning resources, and in instructional design, the school library media specialist encourages the use of technology as an agent of active, constructive learning. The school library media specialist can also use technology to design information-rich electronic learning activities that foster creative and innovative uses of technological formats and that help students become critical consumers of information in electronic form. An advocate for using technology to meet the learning needs of all students, the library media specialist also works collaboratively with both experienced teachers and novices to select appropriate technology as resources.

Goals for the School Library Media Specialist

1. Build and maintain expertise in assessing various technology products and processes for their potential to enhance learning

2. Guide and assist the learning community in the use of new media and technologies for learning and teaching and in evaluating and selecting appropriate informational and instructional resources

3. Work collaboratively with teachers and others to use the principles of instructional design to create, implement, evaluate, and revise information-based learning activities

4. Model and promote effective uses of technology for learning and teaching

Principle 10   The library media program is an essential link to the larger learning community.
A central goal of the school library media program is to promote every student's participation in the learning community—a web of people of all ages, races, abilities, and positions around the world who are interconnected in a lifelong quest to understand and meet

Source: American Library Association photo by Leslie Slavin. Courtesy of the National Library Power Program.

constantly changing information needs. The school library media program acts as an essential link to that community by

- providing physical and intellectual access to information in all formats and at all levels
- demonstrating the fundamental link between content learning and information skills
- supporting the full range of learners for both independent and collaborative work

With its focus on information literacy and its promotion of a vital and exciting culture of learning, the school library media program sets the stage for students' entry into the larger learning community and for others' continued participation in that community.

The school library media specialist is key in building the school's link to the global learning community. By modeling and supporting self-directed inquiry, the library media specialist can inspire critical thinking, problem solving, and authentic learning. By assuming a leadership role in seeking and providing professional development, the library media specialist promotes the value of lifelong learning. By collaborating with teachers and others to infuse information literacy throughout the curriculum, to plan and implement innovative instruction, and to explore the uses of information technology for learning, the library media specialist ensures that students and others have an essential knowledge base.

Goals for the School Library Media Specialist

1. Create and sustain an environment that encourages information literacy, independent and collaborative inquiry, and lifelong learning

2. Orchestrate access to information resources within and beyond the school

3. Promote relationships with external information sources, such as public libraries, government agencies, and business organizations, in support of learning

4. Update personal knowledge and skills on an ongoing basis, identify and assess the school staff's learning needs in areas related to information, and provide appropriate professional-development opportunities

5. Promote curriculum and instructional development based on the information literacy standards for student learning to equip students with the knowledge and skills they need to participate actively and effectively in the learning community.

Information-based learning is essential to a productive and satisfying life, and the library media program will continue to have a critical responsibility for preparing students to participate fully in the global learning community. As teacher and as instructional partner, the school library media specialist brings a unique perspective and a unique expertise to this task. To support student learning with information products and resources, the library media specialist draws upon the information literacy standards for student learning. These standards are a powerful tool for school library media specialists as they help students become independent, information-literate, lifelong learners.

REFERENCES

Barell, John. *Teaching for Thoughtfulness: Classroom Strategies to Enhance Intellectual Development.* 2nd ed. New York: Longman, 1995.
    Introduces research supporting the integration of higher-order thinking skills in schools, presents scenarios of educational environments that foster thoughtfulness, and examines ways of actualizing such environments. Uses actual examples from various schools to illustrate problem-based learning possibilities.
Barron, Daniel D. "The School Library Media Specialist as Instructional Consultant." *School Library Media Activities Monthly* 8, no. 4 (1991): 48–50.
    Discusses the instructional consultant role of the library media specialist and argues that the term "instructional partner" more accurately defines this concept. Reviews professional and educational literature on this subject and applies a business consultant's personal recommendations to the library media specialist's instructional consultant role.
Breivik, Patricia Senn, and J. A. Senn. *Information Literacy: Educating Children for the 21st Century.* New York: Scholastic, 1994.
    Explores a wide range of methods for increasing the information literacy of youngsters and suggests a number of methods for introducing and developing the skills that students need to function effectively in an information-rich society. Discusses related issues like the need for effective staff development and elimination of fixed library schedules.

Brock, Kathy Thomas. "Developing Information Literacy Through the Information Intermediary Process: A Model for Teacher–Librarians and Others." *Emergency Librarian* 22 (Sept./Oct. 1994): 16–20.

Reports on a study designed to formulate a literature-based model that describes what teacher–librarians do as they help students in information search and use.

Brooks, Jacqueline Grennon and Martin G. Brooks. *In Search of Understanding; The Case for Constructivist Classrooms.* Alexandria, Va.: Association for Supervision and Curriculum Development, 1993.

Provides the rational and goals of constructivism; addresses such issues as organizing curriculum by themes, promoting in-depth learning, using multiple resources for learning.

Callison, Daniel, Joy McGregor, and Ruth Small. *Instructional Interventions for Information Use: Papers of the 6th Treasure Mountain Research Retreat,* Troutdale, Oregon, March 31–April 1, 1997. Castle Rock, Colo.: Hi Willow Research and Publishing, 1998.

Major papers by both researchers and practitioners in the field review what is currently known about information literacy and how research should be and is reflected in practice.

Callison, Daniel. "School Library Media Programs and Free Inquiry Learning." *School Library Journal* 32, no. 6 (1986): 20–24.

Provides a method for conducting resource-based teaching as a cooperative activity between the teacher and the library media specialist that will encourage growth and development of inquiry learning (student questioning and discovery of information).

Cole, Robert, ed. *Educating Everybody's Children: Diverse Teaching Strategies for Diverse Learners: What Research and Practice Say about Improving Achievement.* Alexandria, Va.: Association for Supervision and Curriculum Development, 1995.

Discusses use of thematic curriculums to accommodate individual learning styles. Includes teacher-tested strategies to help increase achievement in reading, writing, mathematics, and oral communication. Applications demonstrate sensitivity to diverse cultural, ethnic, and linguistic needs of learners.

Cornelio, Alicia. "A Multimedia Approach to Teaching Library Research Skills." *School Library Media Activities Monthly* 10, no. 6 (February 1994): 38–40.

Describes activities and procedures developed to teach library research skills to grades five through eight using multimedia instruction. Highlights include library media skills objectives, curriculum objectives, resources, instructional roles, hardware and software requirements, evaluation, and follow-up.

Cortes, Carlos E. "Media Literacy: An Educational Basic for the Information Age." *Education and Urban Society* 24, no. 4 (Aug. 1992): 489–97.

Argues that school-based media provide information, help organize information and ideas, help create values and attitudes, help shape expectations, and provide models for action. Suggests that schools should

continuously involve students in analyzing media message systems to help
them develop critical thinking.

Craver, Kathleen W. "The Changing Instructional Role of the High School Library
Media Specialist: 1950–84." *School Library Media Quarterly* 14, no. 4 (1986):
183–92.

Provides a summary of the research literature that documents the changing
responsibilities of the library media specialist.

———. *Teaching Electronic Literacy.* Westport, Conn.: Greenwood Press, 1997.

Provides theoretical and practical information to help library media
specialists teach concepts and strategies for the electronic age.

Dick, Walter, and Lou Carey. *The Systematic Design of Instruction.* 4th ed. New
York: HarperCollins College Publishing, 1996.

Describes the basic concepts and processes of instructional development.

Eisenberg, Michael B., and Michael K. Brown. "Current Themes Regarding
Library and Information Skills Instruction: Research Supporting and Research
Lacking." *School Library Media Quarterly* 20, no. 2 (1992): 103–10.

Reviews research that addresses four major themes about library and
information skills instruction in library media programs. Addresses the value
and content of library and information skills instruction; teaching library
skills in context of the curriculum; and alternative methods for teaching
library media skills.

Eisenberg, M. B., & Berkowitz, R. E. *Information Problem Solving: The Big Six
Skills Approach to Library & Information Skills Instruction.* Norwood, N.J.:
Ablex, 1988.

Provides an information literacy model that focuses on information
problem solving, demonstrates how the model is woven into an information
skills curriculum, and presents examples of integrated curriculum units.

Fosnot, Catherine Twomey, ed. *Constructivism: Theory, Perspectives, and Practice.*
New York: Teachers College Press, 1996.

Comprehensive text that gives insightful background on constructivism, its
ties with earlier theories, important features of the theory, and concrete
applications of it in classroom practice.

Garland, Kathleen. The Information Search Process: A Study of Elements
Associated with Meaningful Research Tasks. *School Libraries Worldwide* 1,
no. 1 (January 1995): 41–53.

Summarizes a study of high school students; results identified five
elements related to satisfaction with the research process and with academic
achievement: student choice of topic, group work, course-related topics,
clarity of goals and means of assessment, and attention to intermediate steps
in the research process as well as the product.

Handler, Marianne G., and Ann S. Dana. *Hypermedia as a Student Tool: A Guide
for Teachers.* 2nd ed. Englewood, Colo.: Libraries Unlimited, 1998.

Shows how to create learning environments that encourage student
collaboration and creativity. Presents ideas on helping students become expert
hypermedia authors and designers while they learn in subject areas across the
curriculum.

Harada, Violet H., and Joan Yoshina. "Improving Information Search Process Instruction and Assessment through Collaborative Action Research." *School Libraries Worldwide* 3, no. 2 (July 1997): 41–55.

  Describes an elementary school team's efforts to improve student academic achievement and critical thinking in the information search process. The authors identify their action research process and detail the intervention and assessment strategies used in the classrooms and library media center.

Harper, Joan. "The Teacher–Librarian's Role in Literature-Based Reading and Whole Language Programs." *Emergency Librarian* 17, no. 2 (1989): 17–18, 20.

  Argues that language programs should result not only in competent language use but also in reading for enjoyment. Discusses the advantages of a whole language approach and includes strategies for incorporating this approach into traditional programs by developing literature-based reading units as extensions of basal readers.

Harris, Judi. *Design Tools for the Internet-supported Classroom*. Alexandria, Va.: Association for Supervision and Curriculum Development, 1998.

  Guides the planning for integrating use of the Internet into the teaching/learning situation in productive, instructive ways that follow instructional design models.

Hasselbring, Ted S. "Using Media for Developing Mental Models and Anchoring Instruction." *American Annals of the Deaf* 139 (Special Issue: Report on a National Symposium, Educational Applications of Technology for Deaf Students 1994): 36–44.

  Discusses two approaches to designing and studying integrated media applications, relating each to current theories of learning and thinking. Examines curricula in the context of new and revised goals for learning.

Heller, Norma. *Projects for New Technologies in Education: Grades 6–9*. Englewood, Colo.: Libraries Unlimited, 1994.

  Provides projects and worksheets using the technological tools introduced in *New Technologies for Education: A Beginner's Guide* (Englewood, Colo.: Libraries Unlimited, 1993) by Ann E. Barron and Gary W. Orwig. Focuses on using technology to support the research process rather than as an end in itself and includes teaching strategies and lesson plans.

Hill, Suzanne. "Information Literacy: Outcomes of the School Library Media Program." *Building Effective Teaching Through Educational Research* (BETTER) Series. Baltimore, Md.: Maryland State Department of Education, 1997.

  Presents current research about information literacy instruction as well as about cognitive approaches to instruction in general. Illustrates how information literacy supports effective learning.

Ivers, Karen S., and Ann E. Barron. *Multimedia Projects in Education: Designing, Producing and Assessing*. Englewood, Colo.: Libraries Unlimited, 1997.

  Carefully reviews each step of the process of implementing multimedia project activities within the school curriculum.

Johnson, Lucille, and Merrilyn Smith. "Library Power and Reading Motivation Programs." Louisiana Library Association (LLA) *Bulletin* 57 (Winter 1995): 179–81.

Presents examples of successful reading motivation programs in East Baton Rouge Parish schools.

Kemp, Jerrold E., Gary R. Morrison, and Steven M. Ross. *Designing Effective Instruction.* 2nd ed. Upper Saddle River, N.J.: Merrill/Prentice Hall, 1998.

Describes the basic concepts and procedures of instructional design, including extensive information on evaluation and assessment.

King, Patricia M., and Karen Strohm Kitchener. *Developing Reflective Judgment: Understanding and Promoting Intellectual Growth and Critical Thinking in Adolescents and Adults.* San Francisco: Jossey-Bass, 1994.

Presents a model of reflective judgment, which desribes a developmental progression in assumptions by adolescents and young adults about how and why they can know.

Kozma, Robert B. "The Influence of Media on Learning: The Debate Continues." *School Library Media Quarterly* 22, no. 4 (1994): 233–39.

Argues the value of exploring how media influence learning rather than continuing to debate whether media influence learning. Uses a constructivist perspective to ground a theory of media and learning in the processes by which knowledge is constructed and the ways that media enhance these processes.

Krashen, Stephen. *The Power of Reading: Insights from the Research.* Englewood, Colo.: Libraries Unlimited, 1993.

Summarizes research on various aspects of Free Voluntary Reading (FVR) from the early 1900s to the present and suggests ways FVR may be implemented. Also explores the limits of FVR, when direct instruction is most effective, and the effects of television viewing on literacy.

Kuhlthau, Carol C. "Implementing a Process Approach to Information Skills: A Study Identifying Indicators of Success in Library Media Programs." *School Library Media Quarterly* 22, no.1 (1993): 11–18.

Demonstrates that the process approach to information skills is based on the constructivist approach to learning. Presents a case study of the implementation of such a program as evidence of the approach as well as a means for identifying the inhibitors and enablers for successful implementation.

———. "The Process of Learning from Information." *School Libraries Worldwide* 1, no. 1 (1995): 1–12.

Presents the process of learning from information as the key concept for the library media center in the information age school. Describes the Information Search Process Approach as a model for developing information skills fundamental to information literacy.

Lamb, Annette. *Building Treehouses for Learning: Technology in Today's Classroom.* Emporia, Kan.: Vision to Action Publishing, 1997.

Presents a lively discussion of the design and development of effective resources and techniques for integrating technology into the learning process. Provides applications and activities using a variety of technology tools.

Lamb, Annette, Nancy Smith, and Larry Johnson. *Surfin' the Internet: Practical Ideas from A to Z.* rev ed Emporia, Kan.: Vision to Action Publishing, 1998.
  Contains interdisciplinary thematic units, subject area activities, lesson and project ideas and information exploration ideas in this practical guide for integrating Internet use into learning activities in Grades K–12.

Leshin, Cynthia B. *Internet Adventures: Integrating the Internet into the Curriculum.* Boston: Allyn & Bacon, 1998.
  Offers ideas on how to teach search skills for Internet use, how to find and join or set up new collaborative projects, how to utilize the Internet in interdisciplinary units correlated to educational frameworks and standards.

Loerke, Karen, and Dianne Oberg. "Working Together to Improve Junior High Research Instruction: An Action Research Approach." *School Libraries Worldwide* 3, no. 2 (July 1997): 56–67.
  A team composed of four science teachers and the library media specialist describe teaching a library research process to junior high students through seven cycles of planning, acting, observing, and reflecting. They report that students experienced the thoughts and feelings identified in Carol Kuhlthau's model of the Information Search Process and also recommend interventions for providing guided instruction.

Loertscher, David V. "Treasure Mountain IV. The Power of Reading: The Effect of Libraries and Reading Promotion on Reading Competence." *School Library Media Annual* 12 (1994): 198–99.
  Describes two Treasure Mountain IV conferences that brought practitioners together with researchers to discuss evidence that library media programs make a difference in academic achievement.

Mancall, J.C., S.L. Aaron, and S.A. Walker. "Educating Students to Think: The Role of the School Library Media Program." *School Library Media Quarterly* 15, no. 1 (1986): 18–27.
  Identifies and explains the role of the school library media program in teaching students to think and describes the nature, importance, and details of this role.

McGregor, Joy H. "Cognitive Processes and the Use of Information: A Qualitative Study of Higher-Order Thinking Skills Used in the Research Process by Students in a Gifted Program." *School Library Media Annual* 12 (1994): 124–31.
  Describes how the use of higher-order thinking skills relates to the information search process and presents findings that support the need to place as much emphasis on thinking processes as on final product in resource-based programs.

Mendrinos, Roxanne. *Building Information Literacy Using High Technology: A Guide for Schools and Libraries.* Englewood, Colo.: Libraries Unlimited, 1994.
  Provides a practical introduction to the concepts and importance of information literacy and high technology resource-based learning. Describes procedures for going on-line and for using on-line databases, telecommunications, and CD-ROM technology in the educational environment.

Montgomery, Paula Kay. "Cognitive Style and the Level of Cooperation between the Library Media Specialist and Classroom Teacher." *School Library Media Quarterly* 19, no. 3 (1991): 185.

Summarizes a study that investigated cooperation between library media specialists and classroom teachers that found that differences in cognitive styles of library media specialists were related to perceived levels of cooperation (between teachers and library media specialist) when planning and teaching library media skills.

Neuman, Delia. "High School Students' Use of Databases: Results of a National Delphi Study." *Journal of the American Society for Information Science* 46, no. 4 (1995): 284–98.

Reports findings based on data from an expert panel of 25 library media specialists. Explains that the major issues related to schools' use of on-line and CD-ROM databases involve their role in students' development of the higher-order thinking skills necessary to plan, design, and conduct research.

Newmann, Fred M., et al. *Authentic Achievement: Restructuring Schools for Intellectual Quality.* San Francisco: Jossey-Bass, 1996.

Summarizes the findings of a federally funded study that focused on the links between effective restructuring efforts and student academic achievement. In their investigation of 24 elementary and secondary schools, the research team discovered that efforts failed when structure and technique were emphasized instead of the "intellectual quality" of teaching and learning. They provide examples of and recommend standards for quality learning.

Pappas, Marjorie L. "Designing Authentic Learning." *School Library Media Activities Monthly* 14, no. 6 (February 1998): 29–31, 42.

Distinguishes between traditional and authentic learning and how shifting to the latter requires teachers to become coaches and facilitators and students to take more active responsibility for their learning. Also highlights the need for a flexibly scheduled library media center, for multiple modes of assessment, and for access to a range of resources.

Perkins, David. *Smart Schools: From Training Memories to Educating Minds.* New York: Macmillan, 1992.

Based on Harvard University's Project Zero, the book discusses the restructuring of curriculum that focuses on critical thinking; learning that is placed in a problem-solving, real life context; studies that challenge students to delve deeply into content knowledge; and teaching and learning that are highly interactive with many opportunities for learners' choices.

Pickard, Patricia W. "The Instructional Consultant Role of the School Library Media Specialist." *School Library Media Quarterly* 21, no. 3 (1993): 115–22.

Focuses on whether library media specialists see the consultative role as important and whether these same specialists actually practice this role. Notes that a much smaller percentage practice the consultative role than think it important and identifies the lack of opportunity to participate in the school's curriculum planning committee as a significant barrier to the practice of the consultative role.

Piersma, Mary L., and Diane D. Allen. "A Revitalized Role for Library Media Specialists in School Reading Programs." *Reading Horizons* 33, no. 4 (1993): 347–58.

Determines the role of elementary and secondary library media specialists in (1) promoting reading growth, (2) assisting classroom teachers, and (3) teaching reading skills and strategies. Compares actual and ideal responsibilities of library media specialists.

Pitts, J.M., J.H. McGregor, and B.K. Stripling, eds. "Mental Models of Information: The 1993–94 AASL/Highsmith Research Award Study." *School Library Media Quarterly* 23, no.3 (1996): 177–84.

Presents Pitts's doctoral research on how students solve information problems, especially in terms of their bringing prior knowledge about information-seeking and using it to help them with their task. Reports on a study that reveals the importance of students having mental models that represent the research process.

Salomon, Gavriel, and David N. Perkins. "Rocky Roads to Transfer: Rethinking Mechanisms of a Neglected Phenomenon." *Educational Psychologist* 24, no. 2 (1989): 113–42.

Reports findings on transfer and non-transfer in such areas as literacy-related cognitive skills. Notes that transfer procedures are learned from extensive and varied practice, while the transfer of conceptual knowledge appears to occur through the intentional abstraction of a concept from one context to a new one.

Solomon, Paul. "Children, Technology, and Instruction: A Case Study of Elementary School Children Using an On-line Public Access Catalog (OPAC)." *School Library Media Quarterly* 23, no. 1 (1994): 43–51.

Focuses on the context in which elementary school children learn to use an OPAC, making it clear that learning to use the electronic catalog comes more easily to those students who are learning the concepts and terms associated with their assigned inquiry, thus learning something about the search process as a whole.

Stripling, Barbara K., and Judy M. Pitts. *Brainstorms and Blueprints: Teaching Library Research as a Thinking Process.* Englewood, Colo.: Libraries Unlimited, 1988.

Authors introduce a research process model that emphasizes different levels of critical thinking, from finding facts to generating new concepts about complex issues. Along with the model and research taxonomy, they provide creative intervention strategies for secondary teachers and library media specialists.

Stripling, Barbara K. "Learning-Centered Libraries: Implications from Research." *School Library Media Quarterly* 23, no. 3 (1996): 163–70.

Interprets and translates Pitts's doctoral research into the personal understandings and mental models of adolescents as affected by information seeking. Includes the presentation of the Thoughtful Learning Cycle with an explication of how this model might be implemented in the secondary school library media program.

Thompson, James C. "Resource-Based Learning Can Be the Backbone of Reform, Improvement." *NASSP Bulletin* 75, no. 535 (May 1991): 24–28.

Argues that resource-based learning can serve as the force and the source for the instructional improvement needed in today's schools. Views as basic such ingredients as cooperation for the delivery of top-quality instructional experiences; reading and research skills; books, material, and media related to the school curriculum; and educational technology.

Todd, Ross J. "Integrated Information Skills Instruction: Does It Make a Difference?" *School Library Media Quarterly* 23, no. 2 (1995): 133–39.

Presents research that supports the assumptions that information skills instruction is a vital part of a school's educational program because information skills emphasize problem-solving and processes of inquiry rather than just skills of location and access to library resources; shows that information literacy should be taught in the context of the school's curriculum.

Turner, Philip. *Helping Teachers Teach.* Englewood, Colo.: Libraries Unlimited, 1986.

Presents the formal instructional design process as a practical method for library media specialists.

Vandergrift, Kay E. *Power Teaching: A Primary Role of the School Library Media Specialist.* Chicago, Ill.: American Library Association, 1994.

Examines the expanded teaching role of the library media specialist and discusses the selection and uses of print and nonprint media resources in the context of instruction and learning. The author integrates a summary of computer and telecommunications technologies and presents examples of instructional interventions and curricular units that emphasize the active engagement of the cognitive and affective domains of student intelligence.

Wager, Walter. "Educational Technology: A Broader Vision." *Education and Urban Society* 24, no. 4 (1992): 454–65.

Considers educational technology's role in designing effective instruction. Describes instructional design that supports systematic determination of instructional goals and methods for accomplishing those goals and for assessing success.

Wells, C.G., and Gen Ling Chang-Wells. *Constructing Knowledge Together: Classrooms as Centers of Inquiry and Literacy.* Portsmouth, N.H.: Heinemann Educational Books, 1992.

Presents collection of papers growing out of a research project in four schools in Toronto between 1986 and 1989. Concludes that "in order to achieve the educational goal of knowledge construction, schools and classrooms need to become communities of literate thinkers engaged in collaborative inquiries." Argues that information skills are part of the process knowledge that students learn in this environment and that help them become "literate" thinkers.

Wolcott, Linda L. "Understanding How Teachers Plan: Strategies for Successful Instructional Partnerships." *School Library Media Quarterly* 22, no. 3 (1994): 161–65.

Discusses the collaborative role of library media specialists as instructional consultants to help teachers plan curriculum and develop instructional activities. Addresses the nature of instructional planning, how teachers plan, and strategies for planning in partnership with teachers.

Chapter 5

Information Access and Delivery

Information is the basic ingredient in the active, authentic learning required of today's student. This chapter focuses on how the library media specialist can implement the information literacy standards for student learning to address the information access and delivery functions the school library media program. The content is written from a broad perspective to encourage local adaptation of the concepts.

Historically, the school library media program has been the primary supplier of information and resources for the entire school community. The program plays an even more important role as the quantity of information swells, the number of information formats expands, and the concepts and processes of information literacy grow in importance. Research and practice converge to show that students' mastery of the concepts and skills of information literacy is crucial to their success within school and beyond. By providing intellectual and physical access to information and ideas—whether within the library media center, in the classroom, or from around the world—the program functions as the heart of the learning community for students and staff alike.

As an information specialist, the school library media specialist connects students and others with the information they need to engage in authentic learning. All members of the learning community need accurate, current information to meet learning needs, and the school library media specialist takes the lead in locating information and offering guidance in its selection and use. With a foundation in the professional literature regarding intellectual freedom and in the technological expertise that is central to modern information retrieval, the school library media specialist provides access to a wide range of electronic and other nonprint resources as well as to their traditional counterparts. As the school's leading authority on information, the library media specialist collaborates with all the members of the school community to create an information-rich environment for learning.

Principle 1 The library media program provides intellectual access to information and ideas for learning.

The information age has made a staggering amount of information readily available. Focusing on the outcomes specified in the information literacy standards for student learning allows the school library media program to promote the full range of information types and sources. The school library media program can provide students and others with strategies for intellectual access—finding, judging, and using information—that they can use both within and beyond formal educational settings. By helping its many audiences become skilled in using information in support of active, authentic learning, the school library media program also helps create a community of lifelong, independent learners.

Source: American Library Association photo by Leslie Slavin. Courtesy of the National Library Power Program.

No one is better suited than the school library media specialist to foster intellectual access to information and ideas. Drawing upon well-honed expertise in focusing on *ideas* rather than only on their containers, the library media specialist is a leader in helping teachers, students, and others learn how to gain access to the concepts, facts, and opinions provided by both traditional and technological information resources. Through collaboration with teachers and others in developing learning activities based on the use of information, the library media specialist helps ensure that information literacy permeates students' learning.

Goals for the School Library Media Specialist

1. Maintain current and in-depth knowledge about the complete range of educational and informational materials, about the characteristics of students and teachers, and about ways of matching individual needs and interests with appropriate materials

2. Develop and implement, in collaboration with teachers and others, a collection development policy that provides access to current and appropriate resources for all members of the school community

3. Develop and implement, in collaboration with teachers and others, policies and procedures that provide appropriate access to external resources, such as those available on the Internet

4. Assist students and staff, through comprehensive reference service and such vehicles as bibliographies and resource lists, in identifying appropriate information resources and in interpreting and communicating their intellectual content

5. Design programs and services, in collaboration with teachers and others, based on the information literacy standards for student learning to provide intellectual access to resources that meet learning and information needs

Principle 2   The library media program provides physical access to information and resources for learning.
Physical access to information is prerequisite to intellectual access. The library media program's collection of resources, equipment, and facilities provides a central point of access for the learning community, as its services are not confined to the school library media center or the school day. The school library media specialist organizes and facilitates a physical environment designed specifically to meet the learning and information needs of students, teachers, and others, with an array of educational and informational resources that provide access to information both within the school and in the local, regional, and global communities.

Plans, policies, and procedures developed by the school library media specialist in collaboration with others can ensure that the program has ample space, equipment, and flexibility in scope and scheduling to provide full access to information and learning resources. With expertise in the acquisition and use of information materials and equipment, the library media specialist provides leadership to the learning community in identifying appropriate resources, in securing funding for their purchase, and in managing their use to encourage active learning within and beyond the traditional school day.

Goals for the School Library Media Specialist

1. Collaborate with administrators, teachers, and others to design and renovate library media center facilities and to identify all physical elements, including informational and instructional technology, to be acquired

2. Select the most advanced resources and equipment, both traditional and electronic, that are appropriate for accessing and producing information related to students' and others' learning needs

3. Coordinate the acquisition and circulation of all information and instructional resources, including
   - printed materials
   - realia
   - hardware and software
   - production equipment
   - adaptive resources for students and others with special needs

4. Organize all resources for effective and efficient use, through such measures as cataloging, classifying, and arranging all elements of the collection

5. Maintain centralized systems for bibliographic control, materials and equipment circulation, and information distribution

6. Manage space, equipment, resources, and supplies for the full range of library media programs and services

7. Encourage flexible access to the programs and services of the library media program by developing and implementing policies for scheduling, space management, and materials circulation that meet the needs of students, teachers, and other members of the learning community

Principle 3   The library media program provides a climate that is conducive to learning.

Although the most obvious function of the school library media program is providing access to information and ideas for all the members of a school's learning community, the program's mission has evolved to include encouraging and stimulating learning based on that information. A student-centered program transcends the

Source: Photo courtesy of the Oregon Educational Media Association.

basic function of access and encourages students to develop the full range of information–literacy skills and positive attitudes toward information-based learning. The effective school library media program begins in an inviting, attractive school library media center that extends this welcoming climate to all the program's services and activities throughout the school. This warm and friendly atmosphere invites students and others to learn.

The school library media specialist holds the key to creating a climate that is conducive to learning. Active, authentic learning involves personal construction of meaning, and this learning occurs most readily in a motivating and inviting climate. The library media specialist exercises leadership in making students feel welcome— both because their physical surroundings are appealing and because the library media staff encourages their questions and their enthusiastic participation in using information resources to learn.

Goals for the School Library Media Specialist

1. Collaborate with teachers, administrators, students, parents, and others to create programs, facilities, services, and schedules that students and others find welcoming and appealing

2. Create and maintain an inviting, attractive physical environment within the library media center and in relation to all the physical elements of the program

3. Be energetic and enthusiastic with students and other members of the learning community

4. Organize materials, resources, equipment, schedules, and space to stimulate and support productive and focused learning

5. Promote the library media program as an attractive, welcoming, and essential venue

Principle 4   The library media program requires flexible and equitable access to information, ideas, and resources for learning.

In a student-centered school library media program, learning needs take precedence over class schedules, school hours, student categorizations, and other logistical concerns. To meet learning needs, the program's resources and services must be available so that information problems can be resolved when they arise. Predetermined timetables without other options and practices that limit access to resources on the basis of age, ability level, or other means of grouping can stifle intellectual curiosity and authentic learning. Flexible schedules can also allow the school library media specialist more opportunities for collaborative planning with teachers. Flexible, equitable, and far-reaching access to the library media program is essential to the development of a vibrant, active learning community.

The school library media specialist encourages free, timely, and easy access to the program's services, resources, and facilities for the learning community. In collaboration with teachers and others, the library media specialist designs and carries out policies and procedures that promote the program as the first point of contact for meeting learning needs. The school library media specialist makes the program's resources available for all, regardless of ability, and at any time—with flexibility and creativity within and beyond the school day, including extended hours, interlibrary loan services, parent and community programs, and after-hours remote access to the collection. Flexible access also requires staff, both professional and support, to accommodate scheduling demands and information needs of learners.

Goals for the School Library Media Specialist

1. Work collaboratively with the learning community to develop and implement policies and practices that

   • make resources, facilities, and professional assistance available at the time of learning need through such mechanisms as flexible scheduling, extended service hours, and after-hours technological access

   • reflect principles of intellectual freedom and flexible and acceptable uses of information resources, technologies, and facilities

2. Maintain an environment that meets the information needs of all members of the learning community, regardless of disability or other difference, through appropriate physical adaptations and instructional policies and practices

3. Encourage the widest possible use of program resources and services by making them available throughout the school and through remote access as well as in the library media center

4. Welcome parents, families, and other members of the learning community to use program facilities, materials, and personnel

Principle 5   The collections of the library media program are developed and evaluated collaboratively to support the school's curriculum and to meet the diverse learning needs of students.
The school library media program offers a full range of instructional and information resources that all students need to meet their curriculum goals. Developed in close collaboration with teachers and others, the program's collections reflect the developmental, cultural, and learning needs of all the students. Evaluated and updated regularly, the collections also exhibit accepted and innovative learning theories, effective teaching practices and materials, and current scholarship in the subject areas. Through collaborative collection development and evaluation, the program's collections promote active, authentic learning by providing a variety of formats and activities for linking information literacy with curricular objectives.

With a broad view of the curriculum, extensive knowledge of both traditional and electronic resources, and commitment to serve the full range of students and other members of the learning community, the school library media specialist can direct the design and maintenance of current, comprehensive, high-quality collections.

Working collaboratively with teachers and others, the library media specialist is the catalyst for creating collections that promote curricular achievement and information literacy for all learners.

Goals for the School Library Media Specialist

1. Maintain current and comprehensive knowledge of the curriculum, of students' characteristics and needs, and of instructional and informational resources in the full range of formats and topic areas

2. Collaborate with teachers and others to develop and publicize policies that govern selection and deselection of resources as well as reconsideration of questioned or challenged resources

3. Develop and direct a continuous collection development and evaluation process that focuses on regular, collaborative assessment of teaching and diverse learning needs and the formats and resources to meet them

4. Maintain and use a variety of appropriate, up-to-date tools and techniques—for example, reviewing sources, published evaluations, and selected Internet sites—to locate and select materials

5. Promote learning resources by maintaining and circulating published evaluations of materials and equipment, by establishing opportunities for teachers and others to preview resources, and by soliciting teachers' and students' regular evaluations of program collections

Principle 6　The library media program is founded on a commitment to the right of intellectual freedom.

Intellectual freedom is "prerequisite to effective and responsible citizenship in a democracy." Throughout its history, the library media program has voiced its strong commitment to the right of intellectual freedom for the learning community. The school library media program continues to promote an atmosphere of free inquiry when faced with today's challenges to educational resources. Freedom of access to information and ideas is essential for students and others to become critical thinkers, competent problem solvers, and lifelong learners who contribute productively and ethically to society.

The policies and practices of the professional associations support the school library media specialist's unique role in guarding the learning community's right to access, evaluate, and use information freely. The school library media specialist is a leader in meeting the school's responsibility to provide resources and services that represent diverse points of view and that support and extend the curriculum with current, wide-ranging information. The school library media specialist provides ready access to resources, programs, and services that address the learning needs of students and others and that are free of constraints resulting from personal, partisan, or doctrinal disapproval. Using the information literacy standards for student learning, the library media specialist collaborates with teachers and others to engage students in active, authentic learning activities that will help them become knowledgeable about the personal and social responsibilities that accompany the right of intellectual freedom.

Goals for the School Library Media Specialist

1. Collaborate with teachers, administrators, parents, and other members of the learning community to create and disseminate policies related to freedom of information that are consistent with the mission, goals, and objectives of the school

2. Promote the principles of intellectual freedom by providing services and resources that create and sustain an atmosphere of free inquiry and by serving as an active advocate for intellectual freedom within the school and in the larger learning community

3. Collaborate with teachers, administrators, and other members of the learning community to build and maintain collections that are appropriate to the learning needs of all the students in the school

4. Model the openness to the ideas and the free and robust debate that are characteristic of a democratic society

5. Guard against barriers to intellectual freedom, such as age or grade-level restrictions, limitations on access to electronic information, requirements for special permission to use materials and resources, and restricted collections

6. Collaborate with teachers to use the information literacy standards for student learning to design and integrate learning activities that equip students to locate, evaluate, and use a broad range of ideas responsibly and effectively

Principle 7   The information policies, procedures, and practices of the library media program reflect legal guidelines and professional ethics.

The school library media program is at the forefront of the complex and sensitive issues that surround information and its uses in today's society. As national and international groups draft and apply legal and ethical principles governing information access, intellectual property rights, and the responsible use of information technology, the learning community looks to the school library media program for guidance on these contemporary information concerns. The information literacy standards for student learning—which promote authentic learning based on active engagement with information in all its formats—underscore ethical and responsible use of information and information technology and provide a foundation for the program's policies.

By creating and communicating policies and procedures that reflect the highest legal and ethical standards, the school library media specialist leads in promoting the responsible use of information and

Source: American Library Association photo by Leslie Slavin. Courtesy of the National Library Power Program.

information technology for learning. The school library media specialist also fosters such use by modeling appropriate behavior and by collaborating with administrators and others to educate the school and local communities about the issues and about current national guidelines and district rules and interpretations. Guided by the traditional standards of the profession as well as by evolving procedures and practices, the school library media specialist is an advocate for respecting intellectual property and a guardian of the right to access information for learning by all members of the learning community.

Goals for the School Library Media Specialist

1. Maintain an in-depth understanding of current legislation and regulations regarding access, copyright, and other legal issues that affect the library media program

2. Demonstrate a commitment to the principles of the library profession regarding intellectual freedom, confidentiality, the rights of users, and other intellectual property concerns

3. Collaborate with teachers, administrators, and others to develop and publicize policies and procedures that advocate compliance with copyright and other relevant laws

4. Model ethical and responsible use of information and information technology by observing all legal guidelines related to access and duplication, by ensuring the confidentiality and security of information for all members of the learning community, and by providing equitable access to information and ideas in accordance with the principles of intellectual freedom and the needs and abilities of learners

In summary, the school library media program supplies information and ideas through programs and services offered both within the school and beyond. By providing intellectual and physical access to the full range of information, in a climate that invites learning, honors free inquiry, and respects legal and ethical principles regarding the uses of information and information technology, the program serves as a model for creative, effective, and responsible information use. The school library media specialist is an information specialist who can guide and promote a student-centered program founded on collaboratively designed polices and procedures that provide flexible and equitable access to information for learning. Using the information literacy standards for student learning to help all students—regardless of age, ability, cultural, or other considerations—learn to locate, evaluate, and use information, the school library media specialist assumes a critical role in creating a diverse, dynamic, and vibrant learning community.

REFERENCES

Berger, Pam, ed. "Information Searcher: The Newsletter for CD-ROM and Online Searching in Schools, 1992." *Information Searcher* 4, no. 5 (1992).

Provides information about the use of technology in the school through four special issues for 1992. Offers feature articles, program descriptions, examples of CD-ROM applications, and reviews of CD-ROM products and technology support.

Burks, Freda. "Student Use of School Library Media Centers in Selected High Schools in Greater Dallas–Fort Worth, Texas." *School Library Media Quarterly* 24, no. 3 (1996): 143–49.

Presents results of a descriptive survey that analyzed high school library media center use in one area of north Texas in 1991, determining the nature and extent of student use of library media centers and describing the characteristics of users and nonusers.

Callison, Daniel. "A Review of the Research Related to School Library Media Collections: Part I." *School Library Media Quarterly* 19, no. 1 (1990): 57–62.

Summarizes the major studies that have implications for budgets and collection size, the selection process, and collection policies.

———. "A Review of the Research Related to School Library Media Collections: Part II." *School Library Media Quarterly* 19, no. 2 (1991): 117–21.

Includes subtopics—evaluation of collections, networking and collection mapping, student preferences, and special collections.

Champion, Sandra. "The Adolescent Quest for Meaning Through Multicultural Readings: A Case Study." *Library Trends* 41, no. 3 (1993): 462–92.

Documents the role of the peer group in making meaning from reading information sources as well as the importance of the student-centered learning environment offered by the library media center. Explains that valuable learning (personal and social change) takes place in an environment in which the individual can interact with peers in a variety of literary experiences.

Chen, Shu-Hsien. "A Study of High School Students' Online Catalog Searching Behavior." *School Library Media Quarterly* 22, no. 1 (1993): 33–39.

Demonstrates that the nature and type of students' errors resulted, at least in part, from a lack of general information-seeking and language skills and a lack of understanding of catalog structure. Includes implications for instruction, such as attention to such conceptual aspects as the formulation of a statement of search concepts and objectives.

Daigneault, Audrey I. "The Collection & the Curriculum Go Hand in Hand." *Library Talk* 9, no. 3 (1996): 1–2.

Discusses the effect of a school curriculum on the collection of books in the library media center and looks at the importance of teachers and librarians working together. Covers the impact of changes in the curriculum on library collections, a collection mapping technique, and methods used to acquire data for collection evaluation.

Dervin, Brenda. "Useful Theory for Librarianship: Communication, Not Information." *Drexel Library Quarterly* 13 (1977): 16–32.

Argues that information seeking and using are situationally bound and occur when the student cannot progress through the situation without making new sense out of something, that is, restructuring the knowledge-base. Identifies crucial elements in the process as the situation, the student's gap in knowledge, and the use of the information to make new sense—that is, to learn.

Descy, Don E. "The Internet/School Connection." *Tech Trends* 38, no. 4 (1993): 15.

Discusses changes in the Internet, including new e-mail addresses and discussion groups that encourage participation by K–12 students, parents, teachers, and administrators.

Doiron, Connie, and Cathie May. "Book Power: The Role of Collection Development in Library Power." Louisiana Library Association (LLA) *Bulletin* 57 (Winter 1995): 173–75.

Focuses on collection development and the Library Power Program's emphasis on updating the collection, purchasing materials to support literature-based instruction, and meeting the needs of a diverse student population.

Doll, Carol A. "School Library Media Centers: The Human Environment." *School Library Media Quarterly* 20, no. 4 (1992): 225.

Focuses on aspects of human behavior in physical settings (e.g., personal space, territoriality, privacy, and variety) that can be applied to create library media centers that meet the diverse needs of student users.

Fedora, Arabelle P. "An Exploration of the Scheduling Patterns of Two Exemplary School Media Centers." Ph.D. dissertation, University of North Carolina at Chapel Hill, 1993.

Reports the finding of a qualitative doctoral study that flexible scheduling promotes the consultative role of the library media specialist.

Futoran, Gail Clark, et al. "The Internet as a K–12 Educational Resource: Emerging Issues of Information Access and Freedom." *Computers & Education* 24, no. 3 (1995): 220–36.

Explores issues of K–12 educators incorporating wide-area networking into the curriculum and becoming consumers and providers of materials on the Internet. Addresses decision making, legal problems, and student behaviors.

Gillespie, John T., and Ralph J. Folcarelli. *Guides to Library Collection Development.* Englewood, Colo.: Libraries Unlimited, 1994.

Provides a useful work for school, public, and academic librarians who are building collections in this age of expanded and shared resources. Includes three major parts—periodicals and serials, child and young adult sources, and adult sources—and covers both print and nonprint media in each area.

Holmes, Linda, Cheryl Singer, and Ola Woods. "Flexible Scheduling, Collaborative Planning, and Teamwork Spell Success for Students." Louisiana Library Association (LLA) *Bulletin* 57 (Winter 1995): 168–72.

> Describes the implementation of flexible access programs and collaborative planning between teachers and library media specialists as a result of involvement in the Library Power Program.

Jacobsen, Frances F., ed. "Children and the Digital Library: Special Issue." *Library Trends* 45, no. 4 (1997): 575–806.

> Presents the views of over a dozen researchers and practitioners on a wide-ranging selection of topics related to children and the emerging digital library.

Jay, M. Ellen, and Hilda L. Jay. "The Changed Role of the Elementary Library Media Teacher." *Reference Librarian* 44 (1994): 61–69.

> Discusses changes in the role of the elementary school library media specialist. Highlights cooperation with classroom teachers and administrators, the role of the school principal, actions to initiate change, structuring research for students' success, and sample library instructional activities.

Johnson, Doug. "Student Access to the Internet: Librarians and Teachers Working Together to Teach Higher Level Survival Skills." *Emergency Librarian* 22, no. 3 (1995): 8–12

> Discusses issues involving physical and intellectual access to the Internet. Topics include skills for effective use, the importance of teachers and librarians ensuring full access for students, and a vision of information access needs in the future.

Kuhlthau, Carol C. "Information Search Process: A Summary of Research and Implications for School Library Media Programs." *School Library Media Quarterly* 18, no. 1 (1989): 19–25.

> Pulls together the results of a series of five studies on student perspectives on information seeking in response to a research assignment. Includes Kuhlthau's model of the information search process and implications of this research for library media programs.

————. *Seeking Meaning: A Process Approach to Library and Information Services.* Norwood, N.J.: Ablex, 1994.

> Lays down the theoretical foundations for the process approach to teaching information skills and providing library and information services. Discusses the theories of John Dewey, George Kelley, and Jerome Bruner.

Manning, Patricia. "When Less Is More: Cultivating a Healthy Collection." *School Library Journal* 43, no. 5 (May 1997): 54–55.

> Recommends criteria for weeding the collection and provides justification for reducing collection size in light of electronic resource availability.

Marchionini, Gary. "Information-Seeking Strategies of Novices Using a Full-Text Electronic Encyclopedia." *Journal of the American Society for Information Science* 40, no. 1 (1989): 54–60.

> Reports on a study of elementary school users of a full-text electronic encyclopedia, noting that students had difficulty formulating effective queries and recognizing the relevance of the information they found.

Neuman, Delia. "Beyond the Chip: A Model for Fostering Equity." *School Library Media Quarterly* 18, no. 3 (1990): 158–64.

Argues that library media specialists have a key role to play in ensuring access to electronic resources for all students. Presents a model with four general steps and seven specific ones for fostering equity within and beyond the library media center.

—————. "Designing Databases as Tools for Higher-Level Learning: Insights from Instructional Systems Design." *Educational Technology Research and Development* 41, no. 1 (1993): 25–46.

Reports the particular problems students faced in using a variety of electronic information access tools, noting that many of these problems stemmed from students' knowledge gaps about topics researched and steps involved in information searching.

Parham, Charles. "Recommendations for the Media Center." *Technology & Learning* (October 1994): 66.

Offers tips on making a smooth transition from a print-based school library to one that offers a range of electronic options in the United States. Focuses on the establishment of a basic electronic reference library, including acquiring both floppy and CD-ROM titles, purchasing hardware and software, and training personnel.

Shannon, Donna M. "Tracking the Transition to a Flexible Access Library Program in Two Library Power Elementary Schools (in central Kentucky)." *School Library Media Quarterly* 24, no. 3 (1996): 155, 158–63.

Describes how participants interpret the process of implementing flexible access library media programs in elementary school settings and how these programs evolve over time.

Solomon, Paul. "Children's Information Retrieval Behavior: A Case Analysis of an OPAC." *Journal of the American Society for Information Science* 44, no. 5 (1993): 245–64.

Focuses on the gaps between children's interests and the subject heading terms employed by an OPAC and identifies developmental needs of elementary school children in language and domain knowledge that affect their ability to pursue a productive search in an electronic catalog.

Thomas, Margie Klink. "The Invisible Media Specialist." *School Library Journal* 42, no. 11 (Nov. 1996): 49.

Focuses on the role of library media centers in the integration of information from electronic sources into teaching units and lesson plans in schools. Notes the failure of the "Breaking Ranks" report to stress the importance of library media specialists in restructuring American schools, student-centered teaching and learning, resource sharing, and cooperative collection development.

Van Deusen, Jean Donham, and Julie I. Tallman. "The Impact of Scheduling on Curriculum Consultation and Information Skills Instruction, Parts I–III." *School Library Media Quarterly* 23, no. 1 (1994): 17–37.

Looks at a variety of factors in connection with the recommended consultative role of the library media specialist as identified in *Information Power.* Reports findings that support flexible scheduling and a planning culture that promotes collaboration between the library media specialist and teachers.

Van Orden, Phyllis J. *The Collection Program in Schools: Concepts, Practices and Information Sources.* 2d ed. Englewood, Colo.: Libraries Unlimited, 1995.

Comprehensive, updated text that discusses both the theoretical and technical aspects of collection development in three parts: its environmental framework—collection's link to external educational and informational systems and internal school and media program structures, practical consideration of materials selection, and operations involved in developing and managing a collection.

Walter, Virginia A., Christine L. Borgman, Sandra G. Hirsh. "The Science Library Catalog: A Springboard for Information Literacy." *School Library Media Quarterly* 24, no. 2 (1996): 105–12.

Summarizes research on children's use of electronic information resources, especially Science Library Catalog (SLC). Outlines cognitive theories that have contributed to SLC's ongoing design, describes the catalog itself, explains the continuing research effort based on SLC, and discusses the research results—emphasizing the findings that are most relevant to library media specialists as they seek to develop children's information skills.

Chapter 6

Program Administration

Principle 1: The library media program supports the mission, goals, objectives, and continuous improvement of the school.

Principle 2: In every school, a minimum of one full-time, certified/licensed library media specialist supported by qualified staff is fundamental to the implementation of an effective library media program at the building level.

Principle 3: An effective library media program requires a level of professional and support staffing that is based upon a school's instructional programs, services, facilities, size, and numbers of students and teachers.

Principle 4: An effective library media program requires ongoing administrative support.

Principle 5: Comprehensive and collaborative long-range, strategic planning is essential to the effectiveness of the library media program.

Principle 6: Ongoing assessment for improvement is essential to the vitality of an effective library media program.

Principle 7: Sufficient funding is fundamental to the success of the library media program.

Principle 8: Ongoing staff development—both to maintain professional knowledge and skills and to provide instruction in information literacy for teachers, administrators, and other members of the learning community—is an essential component of the library media program.

Principle 9: Clear communication of the mission, goals, functions and impact of the library media program is necessary to the effectiveness of the program.

Principle 10: Effective management of human, financial, and physical resources undergirds a strong library media program.

> *These principles were identified and developed by the Information Power Vision Committee, reviewed and commented upon by the profession, and approved by the AASL and AECT Boards as the cardinal premises on which program administration within the effective school library media program is based.*

PROGRAM ADMINISTRATION FOR THE SCHOOL LIBRARY MEDIA PROGRAM

A well-run, student-centered school library media program that is carefully planned, appropriately staffed, and imaginatively and efficiently managed is essential for meeting contemporary learning needs. Such a program, with administrative support, makes a significant contribution to student learning. It also serves as the hub of a schoolwide culture of learning that is strong, stimulating, and vital to student achievement. Creative and effective program administration supports authentic student learning and is indispensable to the development of lifelong, independent learners.

The library media specialist has both the responsibility and the expertise for guiding an effective school library media program. As program administrator, the library media specialist applies leadership, collaboration, and technology skills to design and manage a program that is up-to-date, comprehensive, and fully integrated into the school. Program administration supports both the more visible learning and teaching function as well as the information access function in reaching the entire learning community. The school library media specialist often works behind the scenes in this administrative role.

Principle 1 The library media program supports the mission, goals, objectives, and continuous improvement of the school.

The mission of the library media program—"to ensure that students and staff are effective users of ideas and information"—is a key to achieving the school's mission to foster student learning. Information literacy is a basic skill for the information age, and the library media program is at the core of the school's efforts to foster this skill. The goals and objectives of the school library media program, as outlined in Chapter 1 and developed locally to meet specific needs, establish the program's role in supporting the vision of

Source: American Library Association photo by Leslie Slavin. Courtesy of the
National Library Power Program.

the school as an exciting, information-literate learning community.
By focusing on the creation of a vibrant and collaborative climate
for learning, the program supports the continuous improvement of
the school in its ongoing efforts to develop lifelong, independent,
and socially responsible learners.

The school library media specialist ensures that the basic principles of the library media program align with the mission, goals, and
objectives of the school. Through continuous collaboration with
teachers, administrators, and other members of the learning community, the library media specialist creates formal documents—such
as a mission statement, planning materials, policies, and procedures
manuals—that model information literacy and the library media
program within the school's administrative context. By integrating
the program into all aspects of the school, including needs assessments, technological and other planning efforts, curriculum reform,
and other school improvement activities, the school library media
specialist plays a central role in a successful learning community.

Goals for the School Library Media Specialist

1. Develop and implement a mission statement, goals, objectives, policies, and procedures that reflect the mission, goals, and objectives of the school

2. Integrate the information literacy standards for student learning into all formal documents related to the library media program

3. Serve on the school's decision-making body

4. Use appropriate administrative channels to ensure that the library media program is understood as essential to the school's instructional program

5. Participate fully in needs assessments and evaluations related to school improvement and include the results, particularly those related to information technology, into the development of programs and services

Principle 2   In every school, a minimum of one full-time, certified/licensed library media specialist supported by qualified staff is fundamental to the implementation of an effective library media program at the building level.
Skilled professional school library media personnel are the key factor in programs that contribute to student achievement. At least one full-time, certified or licensed school library media specialist and a full complement of qualified support staff are required in a school to create and sustain an effective program (local considerations will often dictate additional professional staff with additional support staff). A successful, high-quality program requires a competent, professional staff who can provide program administration leadership in collaborative instructional and administrative planning, in integrating information literacy into students' and others' learning activities, and in the uses of informational and instructional technology.

School library media program staff include at least one full-time library media specialist who holds a "master's degree in librarianship from a program accredited by the American Library Association or a master's degree with a specialty in school library media from an educational unit accredited by the National Council for the Accreditation of Teacher Education" (*ALA Policy Manual,* 1996, p. 45). Professional staff must also be licensed by the appropriate state agencies. This educational background for the school library media specialist dictates the level of responsibility of the position as both a professional educator and an administrator on the school staff. Qualified staff includes not only a professional school library media specialist but also paraprofessionals who are appropriately prepared to perform clerical and technical duties. The school library media specialist also guides the school library media program staff to update and integrate their personal knowledge and skills for the program.

Goals for the School Library Media Specialist

1. Interact regularly with supervisory personnel within and beyond library media services at district and other appropriate levels to help ensure that the program is adequately staffed with professional and supporting employees

2. Continuously update personal competencies in information literacy, learning and teaching, information access and delivery, administration and supervision, technology utilization, and other areas to fulfill the requirements of a professional position

3. Participate regularly in activities within the district and at other appropriate levels to gain support and feedback for the program and to be aware of efforts and issues beyond the building

4. Participate in performance appraisals, both as a supervisor responsible for other staff and as an employee committed to seeking continuous professional development

5. Be active in local, state, and national professional organizations and in other professional activities to remain current with recent trends and to contribute to the profession

Principle 3 **An effective library media program requires a level of professional and support staffing that is based upon a school's instructional programs, services, facilities, size, and numbers of students and teachers.**

In each school, the school library media staff must be adequate in number and in expertise to provide appropriate, flexible access to the program's resources and services. The number of professional personnel and support staff in each category is not arbitrarily determined but is guided by the school's instructional programs, services, and technology for all students, teachers, and administrators and is accessible for the school's learning community. A full staff of qualified personnel is necessary to integrate information literacy and critical thinking throughout the curriculum in a school.

As a professional educator, each school's library media specialist collaborates with teachers and others to design, deliver, and evaluate information-based activities that engage students in active, authentic learning within the school's instructional program. To meet these crucial responsibilities, the library media specialist focuses on professional issues of curriculum and instruction while monitoring appropriate technical, clerical, and volunteer staff to maintain the efficient operation of the program. Taking the school's instructional program, services, and facilities into account, the school library media specialist can determine the most effective ways to promote information literacy and the integration of the information literacy standards for student learning throughout the curriculum.

Goals for the School Library Media Specialist

1. Analyze instructional program requirements, the number of students and teachers served, and other pertinent features of the school and the program to determine appropriate staffing patterns

2. Advocate appropriate numbers of professional and other staff to meet the learning needs of the school's full learning community

3. Collaborate with all staff, especially the school's information technology staff, to identify and use the full range of technologies required to meet students' and others' learning and information needs

4. Monitor and supervise technical and clerical staff to facilitate smooth operation of the program

5. Provide access for teachers and students to the school library media center and staff throughout the school day and at other times, as needed, to support the integration of the information literacy standards for student learning

Principle 4   An effective library media program requires ongoing administrative support.
Only within an atmosphere of full and active administrative support can the program achieve its mission and goals. The library media

program must attract and maintain a level of administrative support—including an ongoing budgetary commitment as well as the endorsement of its importance to the school's mission—that enables it to foster authentic learning within and beyond the curriculum and to help students and others become information-literate, independent, responsible learners.

The library media specialist assumes a leadership role in gaining the administrative and financial support the program requires. Through collaborating with teachers and others to integrate the information literacy standards for student learning into the curriculum, the library media specialist establishes the program's central role in student learning and demonstrates the need for adequate support for the program's emphasis in teaching and learning and in the acquisition and use of information technology. The library media specialist establishes and fosters relationships that lead to an understanding of the program and support of its goals.

Goals for the School Library Media Specialist

1. Initiate collaboration with the principal and other appropriate administrators to develop the mission, goals, and objectives of the library media program

2. Communicate regularly with the principal and other appropriate administrators about program plans, activities, and accomplishments

3. Participate on the school's administrative team to provide information about financial and other needs of the program

4. Work with the principal and other appropriate administrators to develop assessment criteria and processes for the library media program and personnel

5. Encourage the principal and other appropriate administrators to support the school library media program by communicating to all members of the learning community the program's contribution to student learning

Principle 5   Comprehensive and collaborative long-range, strategic planning is essential to the effectiveness of the library media program.

Comprehensive, collaborative, and creative planning is essential to the library media program's long-term success. Plans are road maps

Source: Library media coordinator examines blue prints for a new library facility with building library staff. Raytown C-2 School District, Raytown, MO. Reprinted with permission.

for achieving program goals and objectives, and ongoing and dynamic planning is required to keep the library media program at the core of the school's learning community. Long-range, strategic plans must reflect the mission of the library media program, support the school's overall mission, and establish the program as critical to that mission.

The library media specialist has unique insights into current and potential uses of information and articulates the vision of an active, extended learning community that undergirds all phases of planning for the program. By using the information literacy standards for student learning as a planning tool, the library media specialist collaborates with various stakeholders to design and deliver services, resources, and activities reflect the needs of the entire learning community.

Goals for the School Library Media Specialist

1. Establish program planning as a priority and devote adequate time and resources to this process on an ongoing basis

2. Participate on committees charged with developing and implementing long-range, strategic plans for the school (such as

teams for site-based management, school improvement, technology planning, and curriculum development)

3.   Work regularly with teachers, students, administrators, and other members of the learning community to develop and implement long-term, strategic plans that align the library media program and the information literacy standards for student learning with the school's goals, priorities, and national curriculum standards

4.   Create plans for the library media program that

   •   define the program's mission and goals and give direction to the allocation, organization, and management of human, physical, and financial resources

   •   shape the roles and responsibilities of all program staff and focus attention on program effectiveness and accountability

   •   accommodate changes in such critical areas as the nature of the school's population and the development and availability of new resources and technologies

Principle 6   Ongoing assessment for improvement is essential to the vitality of an effective library media program.

Ongoing, regular assessment can be used to keep the library media program active, vital, and at the center of student learning. Program assessment is integral to the planning process. It is also essential to ensuring that the program's missions, goals, and objectives stay current and student-centered and that the program is achieving them efficiently and effectively. Assessment is collaborative and based on sound principles related to learning and teaching, information literacy, and program administration. Above all, assessment focuses on how well the program fosters students' learning and their development into active, independent members of the learning community who use information effectively, creatively, and responsibly.

   The library media specialist provides leadership in assessing the information needs of the learning community and in assessing how well each facet of the library media program meets those needs. In close collaboration with teachers, students, administrators, and other members of the learning community, the library media specialist develops and implements an assessment cycle that guarantees continuing attention to the critical role of the program and its services within the school. The library media specialist's assessment plan follows specific, formal steps to focus attention on a variety of issues: student learning, the place of the information literacy standards for student learning within the curriculum, the role of information technology in the school, the quality of facilities and resources, and the quality and relevance of policies and procedures.

Goals for the School Library Media Specialist

1. Remain current on all issues related to the use of information and information technology for learning and on methods and tools for assessing library media programs

2. Collaborate with teachers, students, administrators, and others to develop and implement a comprehensive plan for identifying the information needs of the school community and assessing the program's role in meeting them

3. Schedule regular, systematic data collection from a wide range of users and potential users of the library media program

4. Use both quantitative and qualitative methods (e.g., both statistical information and observations and interviews) and both input and output measures to collect and analyze assessment data

5. Make decisions based on the results of data analysis to develop plans and policies for the continuous improvement of the library media program

6. Report the results of program assessment on a regular basis to teachers, students, administrators, and other community members

Principle 7   Sufficient funding is fundamental to the success of the library media program.

Creating an information literate society is an expensive task. The school library media program requires a level of funding that will give all students adequate opportunities. In an era when access to information defines the difference between wealth and poverty, the library media program must provide access to all the information and instruction that students and others need for active, authentic, information-based learning. The school library media program requires a budget that supports the continuous collection of information in all formats and that provides the instructional infrastructure that will help students learn to use that information in creative, meaningful ways.

In close collaboration with teachers, administrators, and others, the school library media specialist takes a leading role in planning and managing a program budget that provides for the ongoing acquisition, updating, and expansion of hardware, software, and other materials to support curricular and other learning needs. The library media specialist also presents budget requests that are adequate to underwrite necessary facilities expansion and maintenance and support appropriate staffing and services so that the program can meet the growing and changing information needs of students, teachers, administrators, and others.

Goals for the School Library Media Specialist

1. Work with the learning community to determine the school's information and instructional needs and to develop a budget that provides for the purchasing and upkeep of all resources the library media program requires to meet those needs

2. Administer the budget according to sound accounting procedures to meet all informational and instructional needs and report all expenses as required by local policies

3. Maintain current information on the costs of traditional and electronic resources, on such auxiliary expenses as telecommunications rates and other professional charges, and on sources of funding beyond the school budget for meeting these expenses

4. Investigate and use financial methods and resources to meet the information needs of the learning community, including centralized processing, purchase discounts, partnerships with local organizations, and collaborative grant writing for special purchases and programs

Principle 8   Ongoing staff development—both to maintain professional knowledge and skills and to provide instruction in information literacy for teachers, administrators, and other members of the learning community—is an essential component of the library media program.

Rapid changes in society and technology will continue well into the twenty-first century. The school library media program offers a model of the continuous learning these changes will require. The program's ongoing staff development activities provide a venue for teachers, students, administrators, staff members, and others to learn from one another. Through its commitment to the continuing development of its own staff and its provision of staff development opportunities for all the school's teachers and administrators, the library media program models the active pursuit of up-to-date and accurate knowledge that characterizes the modern learning community.

The library media specialist is both a learner and a teacher in the program's ongoing staff development activities. As a learner, the library media specialist reads the professional literature and attends workshops, courses, and other opportunities to update personal knowledge about the research and practice that guide contemporary education and library media information services. As a teacher, the library media specialist takes the lead in offering regular opportunities for teachers, administrators, and other members of the learning community to explore new methods and ideas, particularly as these relate to information technology and the infusion of information literacy and the information literacy standards for student learning into the curriculum. Through collaboration with researchers and practitioners, the library media specialist pursues the most valuable and current information about learning and teaching, about information literacy, about program administration, and about information issues that are important within and beyond the school.

Goals for the School Library Media Specialist

1. Maintain current and in-depth knowledge of the research and best practices in all aspects of the field—learning and teaching, information seeking and use, program administration and management, advances in informational and instructional technologies, and the implementation of the information literacy standards for student learning

2. Work with members of the learning community to request a staff development budget that provides program staff with adequate opportunities to attend workshops, courses, and other programs to remain current in all areas related to program effectiveness

3. Collaborate with teachers, administrators, and others to identify the school community's learning needs—particularly those related to information literacy and information technology—

and to design and fund staff development programs that meet those needs

4. Offer and promote an ongoing staff development program for the full school community, particularly in the integration of information technology and the use of the information literacy standards for student learning

Principle 9   Clear communication of the mission, goals, functions and impact of the library media program is necessary to the effectiveness of the program.
A well-documented, well-publicized program affirms its own excellence and demonstrates its value to the entire learning community. An effective program increases its stature through regular and systematic communication about its mission, goals, functions, achievements, and overall impact. The information literacy standards for student learning offer a framework for infusing the program's

Source: American Library Association photo by Leslie Slavin. Courtesy of the National Library Power Program.

unique contribution to learning throughout the curriculum and for communicating the nature and importance of that contribution to the learning community.

The school library media specialist is the chief advocate for the library media program and documents its effectiveness so that the full learning community recognizes its value and supports its role. Seeking both formal and informal opportunities to raise public awareness, the library media specialist uses a variety of techniques to demonstrate the program's significance. Through regular administrative reporting, as well as ongoing advocacy, the library media specialist conveys the program's leadership in fostering information literacy, in encouraging collaborative teaching and learning, and in developing sophisticated uses of information technology.

Goals for the School Library Media Specialist

1. Maintain and communicate current knowledge and research findings related to the impact of school library media programs on student learning

2. Report regularly on the program's plans, policies, and achievements to teachers, the principal, other administrators, and parents

3. Develop and maintain an effective advocacy program that demonstrates the value of the program to a broad audience

4. Use a variety of written, verbal, and visual formats—for example, fliers, presentations, displays, and student products—to inform teachers and others of program resources, activities, and services and to promote the program throughout the school and the local community

Principle 10   Effective management of human, financial, and physical resources undergirds a strong library media program.
Efficient and creative management is key to maintaining a student-centered library media program. Strong management skills are required to orchestrate a wide variety of complex technologies and resources and to supervise the specialized staff required to support them. A well-managed program organizes people, funds, equipment, time, and a full range of physical resources and provides the highest level of service to students, teachers, administrators, community members, and others.

The library media specialist develops and implements the policies and procedures necessary for the efficient and effective operation of the program. The library media specialist solicits ideas from students, teachers, and administrators for refining program functions and services and communicates the details of the program's day-to-day operation. Through careful and continuous attention to staffing, budgets, schedules, report writing, equipment maintenance, and other details, the library media specialist supervises and manages the program.

Goals for the School Library Media Specialist

1.   Maintain expertise in strategies and techniques of budgeting, supervision, scheduling, and all other areas of management responsibility

2.   Serve on the school's management team, and collaborate regularly with teachers and administrators through other formal and informal mechanisms to maintain the visibility and quality of the program's management

3.   Report regularly to administrators and others regarding the program's holdings, services, uses, and finances

4.   Participate in hiring, training, and evaluating all program staff, and maintain responsibility for assigning and scheduling staff and volunteers

5.   Administer the program budget and oversee acquisition and use of space, furnishings, equipment, and resources

6.   Oversee all aspects of the daily operation of the library media program

In summary, the school library media program is a key administrative unit charged with unique responsibilities within the school. To meet those responsibilities, the program requires the leadership of a certified or licensed school library media professional, full and appropriate professional and support staffing, strong commitment from the principal and other administrators, and an adequate financial base. The program's long-range, strategic plans and its strategies for continuous assessment focus on providing both physical and intellectual access to informational and instructional resources from within and beyond the school. As program administrator, the library media specialist takes the lead in collaborating with teachers, administrators, and others to build and direct a strong and visionary program that is fully integrated into the school and that meets the current and future information needs of the learning community. The library media specialist clearly and regularly communicates the program's impact on learning, particularly on how the curricular integration of the information literacy standards for student learning helps students and others develop into independent, information-literate learners for the twenty-first century.

REFERENCES

American Library Association. *ALA Policy Manual.* Chicago: American Library Association, 1996.

Baggett, Carolyn. "The School Librarian's Role in Staff Development." *Catholic Library World* 68 (May–June 1987): 266–68, 272.

    Presents several arguments in favor of the involvement of library media specialists in the planning and implementation of school-based staff development.

Barron, Daniel D. "Keeping Current: A Nation at Risk, a Profession at Risk: Will There Be School Library Media Specialists in 2000? Part II." *School Library Media Activities Monthly* 10, no. 3 (1993): 48–50.

    Discusses challenges facing the library media profession during the next decade and the response needed to ensure that the profession continues to exist. Notes the lack of attention to the role of library media specialists in the aftermath of "A Nation at Risk" and the importance of this role as articulated in *Information Power.*

———. "Leadership: Opportunities for School Library Media Specialists." *School Library Media Activities Monthly* 8, no. 9 (1992): 40–50.

    Discusses the need for growth and leadership in the library media profession. Presents qualities of a good leader and describes several books, articles, and an institute dealing with leadership.

———. "School Based Management and School Library Media Specialists." *School Library Media Activities Monthly* 8, no. 6 (1992): 47–50.

    Explains the theory of school based management and suggests implications for library media specialists. Describes the roles of teachers and administrators and the impact of school based management on standards of accreditation and performance-based guidelines.

———. "School Library Media Program Research and Assessment." *School Library Media Activities Monthly* 9, no. 10 (1993): 48–50.

    Reviews recent resources for assessing library media programs and discusses the importance of program assessment. Describes circulation statistics and personal approaches to assessment and discusses the findings of three research reports on the effectiveness of library media programs.

Bennett, Jack, and Frank Brocato. "The Budgetary Role of the Media Specialist in the Restructured School." *Tech Trends* 36 (1991): 39–42.

Discusses the role of the library media specialist in the budgeting aspects of site-based management. Describes the involvement of businesses in education, restructuring school systems through site-based management, and the economic recession and the resulting decline in money for education.

Boardman, Edna M. "Gifts on the Shelf." *American School Board Journal* 177, no. 4 (1990): 43.

Argues that one way to channel support to schools from local businesses is to invite them to donate funds to school libraries. Notes that soliciting the assistance of businesses also increases the number of supporters within the community.

Bruning, Michael. "Is Money Spent on Libraries a Wise Investment?" *Ohio Media Spectrum* 46, no. 3 (1994): 18–20.

Evaluates the achievement levels of students in the top fifty and bottom fifty Ohio school districts in terms of the amount spent per pupil on instruction and the proportion of instructional expenditures committed to the school libraries. Demonstrates that a positive correlation exists between commitment to the library through funding and student achievement levels.

Carson, Ben B., and Jane Bandy Smith. *Renewal at the Schoolhouse: Management Ideas for Library Media Specialists and Administrators.* Englewood, Colo.: Libraries Unlimited, 1993.

Discusses key management issues relating to motivating personnel, short-term and long-term planning, dealing with change and its effects on staff, priority-setting and time management, and communicating with various publics.

Crowley, John D. *Developing a Vision; Strategic Planning and the Library Media Specialist.* Westport, Conn.: Greenwood Press, 1994.

Applies the strategic planning process to the library media program.

DeCal, Ruth. *The Library Copyright Guide.* Washington, D.C.: AECT Copyright Information Services, 1992.

Gives background information, guidelines, statutory references and other interpretive information relating to compliance with the Copyright Act of 1976. Written especially for library media specialists.

Easun, Sue. "Beginner's Guide to Efficiency Measurement." *School Library Media Quarterly* 22, no. 2 (1994): 103.

Introduces data envelopment analysis (DEA), a relatively new efficiency measurement model, and explains its use as a tool for measuring efficiency empirically by identifying combinations of inputs and outputs that allow an organization to achieve as much of its production potential as possible.

Everhart, Nancy. *Evaluating the School Library Media Center: Analysis Techniques and Research Practices.* Englewood, Colo.: Libraries Unlimited, Summer, 1998.

Offers practical guidelines and ready-to-use forms for evaluating a school library media center. Includes conducting surveys, collecting statistics, using observation and drawing conclusions, as well as directions for assessing information literacy with rubrics.

Farmer, Lesley S. "Changing Our Own and Others' Mindsets." *Book Report* 13 (September–October 1994): 20–22.

Discusses the need for library media specialists to respond to changes in the field of education as well as in librarianship. Addresses responses to change, including resistance; new roles for library media specialists, teachers and administrators; cooperation with other libraries; involvement in the school's change process; and library media specialists as change agents.

———. "Crystal Ball Gazing into Library Land." *Book Report,* 16 no. 3 (Nov/Dec 1997): 16–17.

Forecasts some probable scenarios for future school library media centers showing them as community meeting places, learning centers and the most cost-effective means of providing information, research and sharing.

Farmer, Lesley S., et al. "Professional Growth and Development." *Book Report* 13 (November–December 1994): 11–16, 18–19.

Includes four articles that address issues concerning the professional growth and development of library media specialists. Highlights lifelong professional development, mentoring, career development through professional involvement, publishing for recognition and professional growth, professional reading, continuing education, working with vendors, internships, and travel.

Grover, Robert, and Susan G. Fowler. "Recent Trends in School Library Media Research." *School Library Media Quarterly* 21, no. 4 (1993): 241–49.

Takes a broad look at research in the library media field and reports that questionnaires are still the overwhelming research method used in school library media studies and that the overuse of questionnaires is of serious concern. Notes that recent research clustered around five topics: technology, clientele, information resources, the library media specialist, and managing the library media center.

Hamilton, Betty. "Site-Based Management and the School Librarian." *Book Report* 11, no. 4 (1993): 20–22.

Addresses site-based management and school reform, especially the current focus on administrative change in educational reform, obstacles to change in schools, the way site-based management works, and the library media specialist's role.

Hannaman, Kathy. "Library Power and Staff Development." Louisiana Library Association (LLA) *Bulletin* 57 (Winter 1995): 162–67.

Summarizes staff development activities that assisted school teams in understanding Library Power Project concepts to become effective leaders in their respective schools.

Hartzell, Gary N. "Public Relations: Building a Strong Image." *Book Report* 12, no. 1 (1993): 11–17.

Includes four articles that discuss building a stronger image for junior and senior high school library media centers through public relations. Highlights building the influence of high school library media specialists, making the library media center more welcoming for students, providing information for transfer students, and publicizing student achievements through a news collection center.

Haycock, Carol Ann. "The Changing Role: From Theory to Reality." *School Library Media Annual* 9 (1991): 61–67.

Discusses the changing role of the library media specialist based on guidelines and recommendations in *Information Power*. Covers empowerment, current training and education for librarians, continuing professional growth and development, facilitating student learning by working with teachers, information processing skills, interpersonal skills, and time management skills.

Haycock, Ken. "Research in Teacher-Librarianship and the Institutionalization of Change." *School Library Media Quarterly* 23, no. 4 (1995): 227–33.

Reviews research in school librarianship and the implementation of change, highlighting the characteristics of effective programs that affect student achievement and have the support of school administrators.

———. "Research in Teacher-Librarianship: The Implications for Professional Practice." *Emergency Librarian* 17 (1989): 9–11, 13, 15, 17–18.

Includes statements of research findings, comments, and references related to the roles of the teacher-librarian, principal, and program coordinator; secondary school programs and facilities; impact on student achievement; continuing education; resources for students; dissemination of information; and personal qualities of teacher-librarians.

———. *What Works: Research About Teaching and Learning through the School's Library Resource Center.* Castle Rock, Colo.: Rockland Press, 1994.

From 600 doctoral dissertations, culls 28 findings relevant to the effectiveness of library media specialists and library media centers. Includes a compilation and commentary on the studies; an annotated bibliography; and author, geographic, and topic indexes.

Helmick, Aileen. "Analysis of Selected Research." *School Library Media Annual* 10 (1992): 77–82.

Analyzes research cited in "Library Literature" that concerns library media centers. Examines censorship issues; information literacy and library skills instruction; reading; the use of technology, especially microcomputers; and comprehensive state surveys.

Jay, M. Ellen, and Hilda L. Jay. "The Principal and the Library Media Program." *School Library Media Activities Monthly* 6, no. 8 (1990): 30–32.

Discusses the role of the library media specialist as a consultant in the area of instructional design and the importance of understanding and support from school principals to carry out this role effectively. Explores the implications for flexible scheduling, team teaching approaches, personnel selection, and the use of information technologies.

Johnson, Doug. *The Indispensible Librarian.* Worthington, Ohio: Linworth Publishing, 1997.

Discusses personnel issues, including job descriptions and evaluation; roles for the library media specialist to play as leaders in the use of technology; recommendations for budget proposals; a philosophical emphasis on the importance of being indispensible.

Kulleseid, Eleanor R. *Beyond Survival to Power for School Library Media Professionals.* Hamdon, Conn.: Library Professional Publications, 1985.

Extrapolates, from actual case histories, recommendations on politics and economics to provide guidelines leading to empowerment for the building library media specialist and school district director.

Lance, Keith Curry. *The Impact of School Library Media Centers on Academic Achievement.* Washington, D.C.: U.S. Department of Education, Office of Educational Research and Improvement, 1994.

Analyzes data about Colorado library media centers to conclude that (1) students with better funded library media centers tend to achieve higher average reading scores regardless of wealth or educational level of the schools and community; (2) the size of the library media center's total staff and the size and variety of its collection are important characteristics that intervene between library media center expenditures and test performance; and (3) the role the library media specialist plays can influence test scores.

Loertscher, David V. "The Future School Library Media Center." *School Library Media Annual* 13 (1995): 78–90.

Presents various scenarios that depict the increasing diversity in library media programs and the resulting implications for automation, materials, personnel, facilities, and services.

———. "Objective: Achievement. Solution: School Libraries." *School Library Journal* 39, no. 5 (1993): 30–33.

Discusses two studies, one that explored the impact of library media centers on student achievement and one that examined the value of voluntary reading. Presents a model developed from the studies that indicates that adequate library media centers, combined with the effective use of resources, leads to higher student achievement.

Lynch, Mary Jo. "School Library Media Centers: Current and Future Statistics." *School Library Media Quarterly* 23, no. 4 (1995): 251–57.

Summarizes national data available for the library media field collected by the U.S. Department of Education's National Center for Education Statistics (NCES), in particular the Schools and Staffing Survey (SASS).

Miller, Marilyn L., and Marilyn L. Shontz. "Small Change: Expenditures for Resources in School Library Media Centers, FY 1995–96." *School Library Journal* 43, no. 10 (October 1997): 28–37.

Presents the eighth in a biennial series of SLJ reports surveying library media center expenditures. Includes details on spending, human resources, collections, curriculum planning, services, and relationships with principals.

Minor, Barbara B. "Research from the ERIC Files: July 1990 to June 1991." *School Library Media Annual* 10 (1992): 83–99.

Describes research from the ERIC database on library media programs. Highlights library and information skills instruction; information seeking; educational equity; use of technology; censorship; library media center collections; use studies; role of the library media specialist; collective bargaining and certification requirements; and training for library media specialists.

Robinson, Pat Folmer, ed. *Planning the Library Media Center Facility for the 1990's and Beyond.* Austin, Tex.: Texas Education Agency, 1991.

Guidelines for planning school library media centers that will be functional and efficient now as well as in the future. Contains a wealth of practical ideas, sample floor plans, specifications and rationale for each.

Sadowski, Michael J. "The Power to Grow: Success Stories from the National Library Power Program." *School Library Journal* 40 (July 1994): 30–35.

Describes the national Library Power Program supported by the DeWitt Wallace–Reader's Digest Fund. Summarizes experiences of thirteen Library Power Program sites throughout the United States.

———. "Staffing for Success: 1994 School Library Staffing Survey." *School Library Journal* 40 (June 1994): 29–31.

Discusses results of survey of state-level school library officials to determine statewide school enrollments; funding; library media center staffing; state-mandated minimum levels of staffing for library media centers; the ratio of students per library media specialist; staffing standards; and technology and changing roles.

Shontz, Marilyn L. "Output Measures for School Library Media Programs: Measuring Curriculum Involvement. *School Library Media Annual* 12 (1994): 165–187.

Describes a study of thirteen techniques used to collect data from library media centers in eleven schools about the library media specialist's involvement in instructional consulting, student use of media programs, and the percentage of students that come to the center. Includes seven survey instruments and data collected from participating schools.

Simpson, Carol Mann. *Copyright for Schools: A Practical Guide.* 2d ed. Worthington, Ohio: Linworth Publishing, 1997.

Covers many issues regarding copyright for both print and nonprint materials and includes descriptions of copyright guidelines for various media, such as the use of scanners and closed captioning.

Wilson, Patricia, et. al. "Principals and Teacher–Librarians: A Study and Plan for Partnership." *Emergency Librarian* 21, no. 1 (1993).

Reports on a survey of principals' knowledge of the teacher-librarian role and proposes a plan to help administrators become more aware of the role and to strengthen partnerships among teachers, administrators, and librarians.

"What Works: The Perceptions of the Elementary School Principal." *Emergency Librarian* 19, no. 4 (1992): 33.

Presents a research finding that elementary school principals generally have a broader conception of the role of the teacher-librarian than do teacher-librarians themselves. Cites bibliographic information for the eight doctoral dissertations on which the overall finding is based.

Yesner, Bernice L., and Hilda L. Jay. *Operating and Evaluating School Library Media Programs: A Handbook for Administrators and Librarians.* New York: Neal Schuman Publishing, 1997.

Targeted at administrators, provides guidance to the school administrator for setting expectations, providing support and evaluating the library media program.

Chapter 7

Connections to the
Learning Community

Authentic learning for today's student is not bound by the text-book, the classroom, the library media center, or the school. By linking students with the unlimited learning opportunities available throughout the learning community, the school library media program provides a bridge between formal, school-based learning and independent, lifelong learning. It helps them master both a solid base of subject-matter knowledge and learning strategies as embodied in the information literacy standards for student learning. In addition, the program's connections with the learning community increase the resources available to all learners in the school and build a base of community support for student learning and for continuous school improvement.

The learning community involves a wide range of human and resource connections within and beyond the school. Like a series of concentric circles, the learning community begins with the school's students, teaching staff, and administration, and then extends to parents and families and to other local community members and resources. Beyond these circles, the learning community connects with district, state, and regional educational offices and agencies and with professional associations and other national resources. Ultimately, the learning community encompasses international and global resources. The library media specialist is key to forging the school's connections with all members of this learning community. In creating and nurturing these links, the library media specialist uses skills in collaboration, leadership, and using technology to bring resources and information together for all learners. This chapter addresses how the school library media specialist uses collaboration, leadership, and technology to forge connections.

The Learning Community

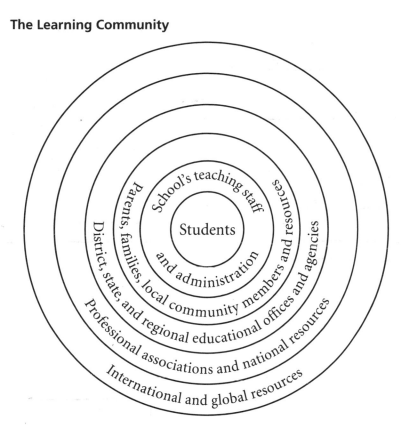

COLLABORATION

The program's connections are grounded in the school library media specialist's collaborative efforts with teachers and others described throughout *Information Power: Building Partnerships for Learning.* Collaboration for authentic, information-based learning—through shared planning, teaching, collection development, and management strategies—provides the model for all the program's connections to the larger learning community.

As a first step, the library media specialist establishes effective working relationships with teachers and the school's administration. These relationships lead to a wider circle: teachers and administrators have ties to colleagues in their own disciplines and to a large number of professional organizations, and they draw upon them for support and for information about new practices and ideas. By forging links with their local instructional and administrative partners, library media specialists also learn from their colleagues' expertise.

Strong relationships with parents and families also lead to a broader network that supports authentic student learning through the library media program. By providing collections, services, and programs that help families foster children's learning, the library media specialist builds a cadre of knowledgeable and enthusiastic adults. These adults not only enhance students' learning, they may also serve as library media program volunteers and promote the program and its role in education to other members of the community.

Links to community resources support information-based learning. Public libraries, museums, and governmental and other public agencies are familiar components of many strong school library media programs; they are especially valuable resources for educational programs and information services. As the National Library Power program, an initiative of the DeWitt Wallace-Reader's Digest Fund, described in the appendixes, has demonstrated, collaboration with public libraries, which serve the school library media program's clientele, is especially valuable for encouraging student learning. Collaboration with businesses and civic organizations also generates personal and physical resources that support student learning. Moreover, the long-term commitment of the community at large to student learning, to information literacy, and to the library media program are invaluable.

School library media specialists also look to colleges and universities for collaborative relationships in support of student learning and program development. Along with the professional preparation of library media specialists, universities are a major source of the research on which solid library media programs are founded, and the library media specialist's active connection to this research is essential. Reading, analyzing, and implementing new theories and practices in the field are critical to the school library media specialist's professional growth and to the development of a vital program. Colleges and universities provide connections to learning theory and research and compilations of best teaching and administrative practices. Action-research partnerships between university faculty and practicing library media specialists can investigate the impact of school library media programs on students' development of information literacy.

District, regional, and state educational offices and agencies provide additional crucial links. They offer special support to school library media specialists in such areas as advocacy, technical services, cooperative programming, opportunities for resource sharing, and leadership on a wide range of issues. They also offer instructional and informational resources to help achieve equitable access to information and to meet learning needs.

Finally, links between the school library media program and national and international groups represent the largest ring in the library media program's interconnecting web. National agencies such as the U.S. Department of Education provide information and services that can enhance the learning potential of every library media program. Professional organizations such as AASL and AECT represent the interests of library media specialists at the national level and provide critical services to support independent lifelong learning. Every member of these organizations has a voice in advocating the library media program as a critical component in developing competent, independent, lifelong learners. Through state and local chapters and affiliates, school library media specialists connect with one another and forge personal and professional relationships that enhance their knowledge of issues, practices, and people concerned with all aspects of their roles.

Collaboration between the school library media program and the other partners in the learning community enriches both the program and encourages communication in all directions. The successful school library media program operates at the center of this active, engaged network of relationships that support dynamic, student-centered learning.

LEADERSHIP

Leadership, like collaboration, is also essential in making connections. The library media specialist strengthens the program's connections by working as a curriculum and instructional leader on the school's leadership team. The library media specialist also acts as a leader in organizing learning opportunities within and beyond the school. By offering programs and services to parents and families, the library media specialist promotes the school library media program as a central resource for the learning community. By connecting with community agencies and businesses to support the library media program, the library media specialist expands resources and forges greater opportunities for learners. By being involved in policies and decisions made at district, state, and regional levels, the school library media specialist promotes the importance of information literacy to student learning across the curriculum. By assuming formal leadership roles in professional associations, the library media specialist promotes the profession to current and future colleagues within the field and serves as an advocate for school library media programs to members of other disciplines and their organizations.

?really?

Schools seek creative and useful ways to serve the adults in their vicinities, and school library media programs are ideally positioned to lead that effort. Providing flexible access and flexible hours makes the library media program's resources and services more available to the learning community. After-hours access to information and resources that are not always available in homes unlocks the door to the school library media program and to the learning community's potential. To provide this access, however, schools need full-time professional library media specialists and adequate support staffing and resources. Programming that focuses on information literacy for the family—reading and book-selection guidance, use of information technology, and other practical skills—turn school library

Source: School board member participates in Log on Day during National Library Week. Reprinted with permission.

media programs into community centers of learning. By designing and implementing instructional programs for families that are based on the information literacy standards for student learning, library media specialists lead the way in helping them learn and use information age concepts and skills.

Community resources, including public libraries, museums, colleges and universities, and local businesses and civic groups, are natural allies of library media programs in fostering learning. These community resources often contribute time, expertise, and funding to worthy causes. By initiating creative community relationships— for example, by organizing mentoring and tutoring programs or arranging for student participation in community projects—the library media specialist can bring the community into the school. By involving students in community projects, such as researching, designing, and creating a neighborhood playground or a community bicycle path, the library media specialist brings the program into the community, provides authentic learning experiences for them, and reinforces the importance of information literacy in real-life contexts.

District, state, and regional activities also offer leadership opportunities for developing effective student-centered library media programs and for publicizing their value to the rest of the community. Educators and politicians at these levels grapple with serious questions about learning in the information age and can look to school library media programs for answers. By encouraging active and forceful leadership for library media services at these levels, library media specialists create a base for developing strong, student-centered library media programs and for publicizing their value to the learning community. By making decision makers aware of the value of library media programs to information-based learning, they ensure that information literacy and library media services are included in funding measures, resource allocation strategies, and legislative initiatives. By advocating library media services to those outside the field, school library media specialists raise the profile of the importance of student learning.

Professional organizations offer another venue for leadership. At local through national levels, they offer opportunities for both formal and informal leadership, from acting as mentors to individual newcomers to prominently advocating such major issues as intellectual freedom and intellectual property rights. By serving as leaders, school library media specialists strengthen the voice of the profession and communicate to the larger community the mission and goals of library media programs and their importance to student learning.

School library media specialists are their own most powerful advocates. Individual library media specialists play leadership roles at every level to make parents and families, members of the community, politicians and educators, and the learning community at large aware of the impact of library media programs on student learning. Strong library media programs are marked by the leadership of library media specialists who build relationships that enhance the program. By promoting information literacy as a key to authentic, lifelong learning and showing how the information literacy standards for student learning can turn that key, the library media specialist exerts leadership on behalf of all the program's constituencies.

TECHNOLOGY

Technology is a primary tool used by the library media specialist to forge connections between the program and the learning community. Technology in this context refers to "the theory and practice of design, development, utilization, management, and evaluation of processes and resources for learning" (Seels and Richey, *Instructional Technology: The Definition and Domains of the Field,* p. 1). It has always played a critical role in school library media programs. Using the concepts and skills embedded in instructional technology, school library media specialists collaborate with teachers to develop and manage effective instruction and to evaluate processes and resources for learning. They jointly create learning experiences that integrate the information literacy standards for student learning with subject-matter content. Using principles of sound instructional design, school library media specialists and teachers analyze learner need, design and implement instruction to meet that need, and evaluate and revise plans for future improvement. This process provides the school library media specialist with the framework for building critical in-school relationships, and it strengthens the program's connections to resources and information beyond the school.

No individual school contains all the resources and information that students need to master to flourish in the twenty-first century. A host of technological devices provides multiple ways to connect the school library media program to the learning community. Computer systems linked through local area networks bring the program directly to students and teachers in their classrooms and laboratories. Electronic mail, listservs, and newsgroups enable library media specialists to reach out and to augment personal, face-to-face connections. Advanced networking and online connections, cable and satellite hookups, and other devices link the school library media program to information resources around the globe. New hardware and software continually expand the options for making connections that support active, authentic, and meaningful learning. Analyzing these options, choosing among them wisely, and using them creatively and appropriately present significant challenges for the library media specialist.

Technological devices also support connections between the school library media program and parents and families of students. As increasing numbers of schools and homes connect to global information services, library media specialists along with classroom teachers can electronically communicate directly with parents in order to involve them in students' learning experiences and to provide information about their children's needs and progress. In addition, school library media programs can provide community access to hardware, software, and instruction in information literacy that help parents and families, especially those with limited resources of their own, to participate more fully in the worldwide learning community.

Technological links to community resources, including public and university libraries, government and other public agencies, and museums, now provide all students with access to previously restricted resources and artifacts. Universities, businesses, and other commercial groups help schools connect with these resources by providing funds and equipment to make the physical links and by offering programs that enable educators to make the best use of these vast and complex resources for learning.

Technological connections to district, state, and regional resources also expand the library media program's connections to the learning community. Distance learning initiatives are available through cooperative arrangements with schools and universities within districts and across states and regions. State and other networks allow rapid and widespread communication of the most current information and foster a dialog that helps to build and strengthen the community. Internet sites maintained by such agencies as universities and state departments of education provide first-line information on topics that have a direct impact on school library media programs. Print and online education publications offer lists of online resources based at individual schools, libraries, and services. Nationally, technological connections allow electronic access both to new resources, such as the Library of Congress's growing collection of digitized resources, and to resources that have been difficult to obtain—for example, the most current figures compiled by the National Center for Educational Statistics and announcements of funding opportunities offered by various federal agencies.

Internet links expand national boundaries to allow connection to an ever-broadening circle to enhance students' and others' learning. The library media profession directly supports several technological connections to the learning community. LM_NET, hosted by the ERIC Clearinghouse on Information and Technology, enables library media specialists and library media educators around the world to share information, to exchange ideas, and to become part of a global professional community. ICONnect, the technology initiative of AASL described in the appendixes, provides opportunities for library media specialists and teachers to learn more about using electronic information effectively. KIDSConnect, ICONnect's K–12 component, allows students to e-mail library media specialist volunteers who guide them toward resources (including their local library media specialists) that satisfy their information needs.

While technological links do not substitute for the human connections that are central to effective learning and teaching, they allow library media specialists to quickly and easily connect with people and resources. Especially by using technology to make connections that are otherwise impractical or impossible, the school library media specialist offers opportunities for students to explore the world and its resources in unprecedented ways. Technology connections allow learners to apply the information literacy standards for student learning and to participate in a community of learners that spans the globe.

Collaboration, leadership, and technology underlie *Information Power* and the vision of a dynamic, student-centered library media program that begins in the school and extends its connections throughout the community, the nation, and the world. These themes focus the school library media specialist's efforts to establish and maintain a program that is grounded in solid research, sound theory, and the best educational practices. Using the information literacy standards for student learning as the framework for thoughtful, information-based learning, individual school library media centers must create their own unique programs for preparing information-literate citizens of the future.

CONCLUSION

Both the lay and professional literature report concerns that schools can no longer follow the design of the past, preparing young people for an industrial society. Instead, we must be preparing students for an information society. What does this mean for how students need to learn and how we need to teach? We must teach students to be learners, because in their lifetimes so much new knowledge will be generated that they cannot expect to stop learning when they leave school. What are learners? They are people who inquire, who seek information, evaluate it, apply it to new problems, questions, or decisions, and assess how well the information has met their needs.

Source: American Library Association photo by Leslie Slavin. Courtesy of the National Library Power Program.

These aspects of intellectual work call for students to exploit the potential of the school library media program as a point of access, communication, learning, and creation. When this kind of intellectual activity occurs, students will leave us ready to thrive in an information society.

REFERENCES

Anderson, Mary Alice. "How to Make Successful Technology Connections in Your Media Center." *Book Report* (September–October, 1994): 3.
    Offers tips to library media specialists on how to make successful technology connections with teachers and students through media programs.
Bandieira de Mello, Victor, and Stephen P. Broughman. *SASS by State, 1993–94 Schools and Staffing Survey: Selected State Results.* Washington, D.C.: U. S. Department of Education, National Center for Education Statistics, 1996.
    Highlights some of the state-level comparisons of libraries/media centers responding to 1993/94 questionnaire. Compares public school libraries/media centers by state, school level (elementary/secondary), enrollment size, and staff.
Barron, Daniel D. "Keeping Current: School Library Media Specialists and the Global Village." *School Library Media Activities Monthly* 8, no. 7 (1992): 48–51.
    Discusses the concept of a global village and suggests 32 resources to help schools develop programs of global education (GE). Highlights general background resources, descriptions of GE programs that relate to specific curriculum areas, and resources that have implications for school library media programs.
Barron, Daniel D. "Learning Communities and School Library Information Professionals." *School Library Media Activities Monthly* 11, no. 1 (1994): 48–50.
    Discusses the concept of the learning organization contained in Peter Senge's text, *The Fifth Discipline: The Art and Practice of the Learning Organization,* and its application to schools. Describes the school library information professional's potential role as a practitioner of systems thinking.
Bowers, C.A. "Technology, Culture, and the Challenge of Educational Leadership." *Teaching Education* 5, no. 1 (1992): 21–28.
    Clarifies some important cultural mediating characteristics of technology and examines the more salient reasons why educational leaders should be wary of using the information age as the justification for promoting wider educational use of computers.
Bracy, Pauletta. "Discovered in North Carolina: An Overview of Research Related to School Library Media Programs." *North Carolina Libraries* 54, no. 1 (1996): 9–18.
    Presents an overview of 15 studies conducted in or about North Carolina related to school library media programs. Highlights the roles of programs and library media specialists as perceived by principals, students and peers; reading interests of teenagers; professional roles in reference services, information skills instruction, and cooperation between public and school libraries; and how technology is used.

Craver, Kathleen W. *School Library Media Centers in the 21st Century: Changes and Challenges.* Westport, Conn.: Greenwood Press, 1994.

Examines and discusses major forces for change facing library media centers and analyzes their implications.

Crowley, John. "A Leadership Role for Library Media Specialists." *School Library Media Annual* 13 (1995): 60–65.

Discusses the role of the library media specialist in education. Highlights strategic planning for the library media center and for schools.

Duke, Jenola. "Community Involvement in Library Power." Louisiana Library Association (LLA) *Bulletin* 57 (Winter 1995): 182–85.

Describes community involvement in implementing the Library Power Program in Baton Rouge and resulting services to the community such as extended library media center hours, expanded adult education programs and services, and storytelling workshops and programs.

Goodin, M. Elspeth. "The Transferability of Library Research Skills from High School to College." *School Library Media Quarterly* 20, no. 1 (1991): 33–42.

Describes a study designed to determine whether a program of instruction could be developed to teach high school students library and information skills that would prove useful to them in college. Indicates that a program of instruction makes a significant impact on students' attitudes and performance but that the transfer of these beneficial effects to undergraduate study is less clear.

Knowles, Elizabeth, and Martha Smith. *The Reading Connection.* Englewood, Colo.: Libraries Unlimited, 1997.

Presents ideas on how to involve parents in promoting literacy to young readers through implementing a book club. Includes selection of materials, topic suggestions and sample book club sessions.

Krashen, Stephen D. *Every Person a Reader: An Alternative to the California Task Force Report on Reading.* Culver City, Calif.: Language Education Associates, 1996.

Answers the California Task Force Report based on his research identifying significant predictors of reading comprehension test scores. Notes as positive predictors the number of books per student in library media centers and the average circulation in public libraries in neighborhoods where the students live.

———. "School Libraries, Public Libraries, and the NAEP Reading Scores." *School Library Media Quarterly* 23, no. 4 (1995): 235–237.

Discusses the relationship between reading ability and library quality and use, focusing on results of a multiple regression analysis of data that examined fourth-grade scores on the 1992 NAEP Reading Comprehension test. Notes that significant variables include books per student in school library media centers, circulation in public libraries, and software available.

Mancall, Jacqueline C. "The Changing Library Landscape: Impact on Student Instruction and Use." *School Library Media Annual* 11 (1993): 66–76.

Discusses changes in library media centers and their impact on student instruction and use. Highlights national guidelines, the National Goals for Education, educational research and reporting, global patterns, information delivery and storage, the projected configuration for libraries and information services, skills for information literacy, and instructional considerations for achieving skill development.

Mancall, Jacqueline C. et al. "Searching across the Curriculum." *Phi Delta Kappan* 73, no. 7 (1992): 526–28.

Explains how future library media specialists will serve as information consultants to students and teachers and as gatekeepers to new information technologies and resources. Argues that library media center services will provide easy access to local, regional, and national collections and highlights two high schools in Maryland and suburban Chicago that are experimenting with information searches across the curriculum.

Mathews, Virginia H. "Kids Need Libraries: School and Public Libraries Preparing the Youth of Today for the World of Tomorrow." *School Library Journal* 30, no. 4 (1990): 33, 37.

Reviews issues identified by the White House Conference on Library and Information Services that relate to the needs of youth and offers specific suggestions for ways in which libraries can meet those needs. Discusses proposed federal legislation and includes a checklist designed to assess gaps at the state and local levels.

Pappas, Marjorie. "A Vision of School Library Media Centers in an Electronic Information Age." *School Library Media Activities Monthly* 10 (September 1993): 32–34.

Discusses evolving trends in schools and library media centers as a result of electronic information technologies.

Robinson, Rhonda S. "Controlling Technology: Facilitating Decision-Making and Empowering Teachers." *Thresholds in Education* 17, no. 4 (1991): 11–12.

Argues that technology cannot resolve instructional problems unless teachers are involved in the technology decision-making process. Explains that educators must perform curriculum, student, and community needs analyses; determine curricular objectives; develop district and school plans; provide cooperative teacher training prior to initiation; and obtain regular feedback for students and teachers.

Rothenberg, Diane. "Information Technology in Education." *Annual Review of Information Science and Technology (ARIST)* 29 (1994): 277–302.

Discusses information technology in teacher education, teaching, and learning in elementary and secondary education from 1991–93. Addresses school reform, the effects of information technology on student achievement, networked schools, telecommunications, information services and technology in library media centers, Internet use, information skills instruction, and future possibilities.

Rux, Paul. "Listening to the Music." *Book Report* 13, no. 2 (1994): 15–16.

Examines issues relating to information technology that will affect the future of library media specialists. Discusses teaching versus learning; the need for new sets of skills; becoming systems analysts; matching technology with user information needs; management information systems; and shifting models regarding the role of school librarians.

Seels, Barbara B., and Rita C. Richey. *Instructional Technology: The Definition and Domains of the Field.* Washington, D.C.: Association for Educational Communications and Technology, 1994.

Addresses developments in instructional technology theory and practice. Reexamines the definition in the 1977 *The Definition of Educational Technology* and addresses the domains, influences on instructional technology, and the practice.

Shantz, Doreen. "Program Advocacy." *Emergency Librarian* 21, no. 3 (1994): 22–23, 25.

Discusses program advocacy in schools, focusing on the role of the teacher-librarian in cooperation with the classroom teacher and the principal. Describes a program in Ontario called "Partners in Action" in which leadership skills are discussed and program advocacy strategies are suggested at the school and system levels.

Stripling, Barbara K. *Libraries for the National Education Goals.* Washington, D.C.: Office of Educational Research and Improvement (ED), 1990.

Reviews and summarizes information about the role of libraries in educational efforts designed to meet the National Education Goals. Argues that libraries must play a pivotal role in meeting these goals, including efforts to prepare students to cope with learning in an information age and the provision of a national electronic network for students, teachers, administrators, and community members.

Trotter, Andrew. "It's Overdue." *Executive Educator* 16, no. 12 (1994): 18–23.

Argues that if students can direct visitors to their library media center, it probably is central to their learning. Notes that budget cuts have resulted in too many understaffed, understocked, and closed-down facilities and suggests that cooperation with public libraries may help bring school libraries into the information age.

Appendix A
Library Power

This document provides background on Library Power, a $40 million national school improvement initiative funded by the DeWitt Wallace-Reader's Digest Fund. The initiative has concentrated on improving teaching and learning through revitalizing elementary and middle school library media programs throughout the country by providing funding, consultant assistance, and both quantitative and qualitative assessment. Of special import to the school library media field is the fact that the Fund's grantmaking proposal was built on the recommendations of *Information Power* (ALA, 1988). Early reports of quantitative assessment and opinions of project directors, school library leadership, and AASL staff involved with Library Power attest to the validity of the components of Library Power, many of which are based on *Information Power* principles. As we move into the next phase of empowering school library media program development with *Information Power,* 1998, the Library Power experience provides the field with data, model sites, and encouragement to support our belief in the vital contributions that library media programs can make to student learning.

In 1988, the DeWitt Wallace-Reader's Digest Fund initiated Library Power, planned as a 10-year, $40 million investment to revitalize school library media centers across the country. After two years of development and testing in the New York City School System, the goal of national expansion became a reality when, in 1991, Library Power was established in several communities around the country. By 1995, nineteen communities had been brought into the Library Power initiative. These nineteen communities had several things in common: they housed outdated school library media centers that were in desperate need of revitalization; they had developed a vision for improving teaching and learning through the library; they were mobilizing community support for their vision; and they had made a commitment to full-time library media specialists, professional development, and flexible scheduling. Library Power eventually operated in approximately 700 schools and affected more than 400,000 students. Library Power is the largest non-governmental school library media investment since the 1962 Knapp School Libraries Project and is bigger in terms of dollars and numbers of students than many other current school reform efforts.

The Fund's summary interest in Library Power was to demonstrate the feasibility of turning large numbers of school libraries into state-of-the-art educational centers that help improve teaching and learning in the nation's schools. Library Power was developed around six goals:

- Create a national vision and new expectations for public elementary and middle school library programs and encourage new and innovative uses of the library's physical and human resources
- Create model library programs that are an integral part of the educational process
- Strengthen and create awareness for the role of the library media specialist as a teacher and information specialist who collaborates with teachers and students
- Encourage collaboration among teachers, administrators and library media specialists that results in significant improvement in the teaching and learning process
- Demonstrate the significant contributions that school library media programs can make to school reform and restructuring efforts
- Encourage the creation of partnerships among leaders in school districts, public libraries, community agencies, business communities, academic institutions and parent groups to improve and support school library programs

The operation of Library Power is organized around these six core activities:

- building resource collections matched to subjects students are studying in class
- operating school library media centers on a flexible schedule so students and teachers can use resources at times best suited to instructional need
- providing and organizing appropriate library media center facilities

- using collaborative planning and delivery of instruction
- staffing the media center with full-time library media specialists
- providing ongoing professional development for all participants

The Fund-commissioned evaluation of Library Power has been ongoing, and the final report will be issued in 1998. Evaluation activities (both quantitative and qualitative) have included surveys, collection maps (mapping how well the collection matches the curriculum of the school), collaboration logs (an ongoing record of collaborative units), and case studies. Although the Library Power evaluation is still being completed, several trends and accomplishments have been derived from the quantitative data analyzed to this point.

RESULTS FROM RESEARCH DATA

1. Improving School Collections

- Collections generally have been improved through emphasis on instructional needs of both teachers and students as well as need for multicultural resources.
- 69% of teachers in Library Power schools collaborate in building library media center collections; 94% feel that collaboration will continue; 99% feel the collaboration should continue.

2. Providing Appropriate Library Facilities

- Three-quarters of Library Power schools now have facilities for individual activities, small groups, large groups, storytimes, and multiple activities including computer use.
- Even though technology was not a focus of the initiative, Library Power schools have increased their access to technology, particularly in the number of computers with modems (46% increase), connection to the Internet (59%), and CD-ROM for full text (43%).
- The most frequently owned (by 80% or more) technologies as a whole in all Library Power schools include: telephone, computer with modem, CD-ROM for full text/images, connection to the Internet, and cable television.

3. Providing Qualified Staff and Other Personnel for the Media Program

- 94% of Library Power schools have one or more professional, certified library media specialists.
- Two-thirds of the Library Power library media centers use volunteers to perform duties that free the library media specialist to work on tasks more centrally related to curriculum and instruction.

4. Providing Access to the Library Media Center

- Students in 95% of Library Power schools have flexible or semiflexible access to their school library media centers using the center on an average of one-and-a-half times a week as an individual, a member of a class, or a small group.
- 65% of teachers in Library Power schools reported an increase in student library media center use since the beginning of Library Power while 60% noted an increase in the use of the media center on the students' own initiative, and 72% described student attitudes toward using the center as more positive.
- Library Power media specialists, principals, and teachers all believe that the practice of as-needed access to the library media center will continue and should continue.

5. Using Collaborative Planning and Delivery of Instruction

- Approximately one-half of the teachers in Library Power schools said that they collaborated with a library media specialist for the planning and designing of instruction, and one-third of the teachers said that they collaborated with a library media specialist in delivering instruction.
- More than 90% of library media specialists, teachers, and principals believe that the practice of collaboration between library media specialists and teachers both will and should continue. This represents a significant shift in attitudes toward collaboration.

RESULTS FROM OBSERVATIONS
OF PARTICIPANTS

Less scientifically collected, but perhaps no less important, are effects of Library Power identified by a number of Library Power directors and school district supervisors—effects on learning, teaching, the library media specialist, school culture, the library media program, and the community. They report the following:

Library Power has empowered many students to be independent learners. Information literacy skills are embedded in the curriculum, and many students have had flexible and continuous access to the library to use those skills. Students are expected to find in-depth information about topics that they are interested in; they are encouraged to follow up on their own questions and to bring that information back to share with their classmates. Learning has become a process of discovery for these students.

These students have developed ownership of their learning because they are making decisions and finding information independently. As their ownership has increased, so has their motivation for learning and their sense of responsibility. Library Power directors in several sites have commented that students who have been trusted to go to the library respond with responsible behavior and higher self-esteem.

Because the Library Power model is built around collaboration, teaching has also been substantively affected in many schools. Teachers are working with each other and with the library media specialist to develop and teach units that integrate content and information literacy skills. Many of these units are interdisciplinary. Some teachers have given up strict control over the learning process in order to facilitate students learning on their own. Some principals have recognized the effectiveness of collaborative teaching and have honed their own ability to lead through facilitation rather than authority.

Many principals and teachers have indeed been affected by Library Power, but the most profound personal impact has been on library media specialists. Most have developed a new, more professional vision for librarianship. The networking available through Library Power has ended the traditional isolation of library media specialists. Increases have been observed in their leadership ability, political awareness, advocacy ability, human relations skills, self esteem, and collaborative planning and teaching skills. Some library media specialists have even become empowered through Library Power professional development to lead their schools in a change process.

The collaborative process and changes in teaching and learning have led to a new culture in Library Power schools. When they have achieved the Library Power vision, these schools have become energizing communities that offer mutual support to teachers, students, and parents through collaborative relationships. Parents use the library as an entree to the school, borrowing materials, learning the use of technology, and learning and reading with their children. The focus brought through Library Power has enhanced the instructional approaches of the teachers, including inquiry learning, literature-based teaching, integration of skills and content, phonics, collaboration, and various forms of assessment.

In this changed culture, the library media program is recognized as the instructional center of the school, a place of comfort and pleasure where students can pursue their own dreams and ideas. Reading and literacy have become important focal points for the whole school. The library is a center for both curricular and personal reading, resulting in greatly increased circulation rates in some schools. In some Library Power sites, the school library media center has even become an educational resource for the entire community, with materials and programs available on technological literacy, careers, and parenting.

Communities have built on their increased access to library resources and the collaborative culture of Library Power to become involved with a few school library media programs in more substantive ways. Community members (particularly parents) collaborate on library media programs, offer tutoring and special help to students, share their expertise and reinforce the learning of information skills with their children. Library Power has helped to create a public will in some communities to offer the best in learning opportunities through the school library media program to their children. In a couple of sites, it has even increased the collaboration between school and public libraries and caused a new focus on children's services in public libraries.

ELEMENTS OF SCHOOL REFORM

Just as observations of Library Power directors and school district library media supervisors have noted some fairly consistent effects on library programs and schools in sites across the country, so have they anecdotally noted elements that have helped Library Power function as a school-change initiative. They have identified elements, that, taken together, provide a model for whole-school instructional reform. Perhaps it is this model of Library Power as a catalyst for school change that will provide the deepest and most lasting effect on schools and school library media programs. The elements of Library Power that have proven to be essential for real change in schools include:

Focus on Integrated Vision

All of the members of the school community should agree on what they expect children to know and be able to do. Then the school has to come to consensus on strategies to help children reach these learning goals. Library Power provides a vision that combines learning goals with strategies for enhancing teaching and learning.

Impetus and Environment for Change

External pressure can provide impetus for change within a school. Parents, business leaders, local education funds, grantmakers, legislatures, higher education institutions, economic realities—all can offer a real-world mandate for raising student achievement.

Even with impetus, the physical and mental environments of the school have to nurture change. Some Library Power sites have discovered that small schools are significantly easier to change. The physical environment must also be flexible. Flexible scheduling, open access to the library, and time for planning within the school structure are fundamental to any effort to make the library a center of learning for the whole school. Attitudes in the school community form an environment that fosters change if members of the community are willing to take risks and are open to new ideas.

Collaboration

The collaboration required for school change goes much beyond mere compliance or cooperation. Participants should expect to work through different points of view, to capitalize on various strengths, and to compensate for individual weaknesses. Collaboration requires full commitment from every educator in the school. In many Library Power sites, collaboration with the community has been especially critical. Although often difficult in the early stages, this community buy-in in some sites has proven to be important for continuation of the change process beyond the grant funding cycle.

Leadership and Support

Leadership is particularly important for any whole-school change effort. The Library Power requirement of a full-time library media specialist for each school has been fundamental to the success of the initiative. Sites have discovered, moreover, that the library media specialist is not the only source of leadership. If leadership is allowed to emerge from the school community, the effort can be led by the library media specialist, principal, teachers, parents, business leaders or a combination.

All Library Power sites have discovered that active and vocal administrative support for the work is critical, especially from the school principal. Administrative leadership provides necessary structures for school change—ongoing professional development, opportunities to participate in and be supported by a collaborative team, a culture of protected risk-taking, and access to peer support networks.

Professional Development

Real school change cannot happen without opportunity and support for professional development. Library Power sites used a variety of structures (e.g., workshops, conferences, consultants, planning time, mentoring, modeling) to provide these opportunities for teachers, administrators, and library media specialists. No matter what structures were used, however, sites discovered that changes in practice resulted from professional development that was sustained and intensive.

New Roles

During a change process, those participating discover that they have to learn new roles. Many principals, teachers, library media specialists, parents, and even students have assumed new responsibilities as they have focused on raising student achievement. These principals have delegated management tasks in order to assume the role of instructional leader. Teachers have learned teamwork and collaboration in instructional design and teaching. Some library media specialists have delegated technical and administrative work in order to take responsibility for the content learning and information literacy skills of students. Some parents have participated in the evaluation of student work and long-range planning for the library and school. Students have assumed responsibility for their own learning.

Resources

Additional resources have a substantial impact on facilitating change. In Library Power, the grant funding has allowed schools to purchase collections that match the curriculum and make independent learning possible. New or renovated library facilities make the library media center exciting, inviting places to learn, think and enjoy reading. They invite students to discover new ideas and information on their own. Technology and electronic resources have taken a prominent place as integral components of the library media program. The Library Power resources have leveraged additional funding, both public and private, in sites across the country.

Time

Time is a critical element in any school-change process. Schools will evolve at different rates, depending on where they are in the process. Every school will have times of seemingly rapid change when several structures or strategies are implemented at once. At other times there will be no visible signs of change because participants are learning, adopting, and adapting the ideas. School change pivots on the modification of attitudes and that takes time.

Accountability

Inherent in any school-change effort is the necessity for evaluating results. Most Library Power sites have discovered that reflection adds an essential component of thoughtfulness to the change process. Sites have tried different evaluation methods, including surveys, written comments, portfolios, evaluation scales or rubrics, examination of collaborative units, collection of data by schools, and research conducted by non-participant researchers. Once the evaluation has been completed, accountability demands that the public be engaged in an examination of lessons learned. Public engagement and dissemination of results are integral to any school-change process.

LIBRARY POWER: A MODEL FOR EFFECTIVE SCHOOL LIBRARY MEDIA CENTERS

If a school is committed to enhancing student achievement by changing its teaching and learning, then Library Power offers a model for the elements that lead to effective change. The dynamics of each situation will determine the sequence and relative importance of the elements, but no lasting change can be achieved without full commitment to a shared vision of learning.

Library Power has been evolving for the past ten years; this quiet evolution has become a revolution. The impact of Library Power extends beyond the nineteen communities involved, beyond the life of funding from DeWitt Wallace-Reader's Digest Fund. The lessons learned have the potential for guiding and inspiring school library media specialists and other educators across the country as they lead their schools to improved teaching and learning.

BIBLIOGRAPHY

The following sources contain additional information about Library Power principles and practices.

Educational Priorities Panel. *School Libraries ... No Reading Allowed.* New York: Interface, 1985. (Available from New Visions for Public Schools, 96 Morton Street, 6th Floor, New York, NY 10014)

Fund for New York City Public Education. *School Libraries ... Unfinished Business.* New York: New Visions for Public Schools, 1996. (Available from New Visions for Public Schools, 96 Morton Street, 6th Floor, New York, NY 10014)

Giorgis, Cyndi and Barbara Peterson. "Teachers and Librarians Collaborate to Create a Community of Learners." *Language Arts* 73 (November 1996): 477–82.

Goldfarb, Liz and Sheila Salmon. "Enhancing Language Arts for Special Populations: Librarians and Classroom Teachers Collaborate." *Language Arts* 70 (November 1993): 567–72.

Hughes, Sandra. *Library Power: A Report to the Community.* Philadelphia: Philadelphia Education Fund, 1997. (Available from Philadelphia Education Fund, Seven Benjamin Franklin Parkway, Suite 700, Philadelphia, PA 19103)

Sadowski, Michael. "The Power to Grow: Success Stories from the National Library Power Program." *School Library Journal* 40 (July 1994): 30–35.

Salmon, Sheila et al. *Power Up Your Library: Creating the New Elementary School Library Program.* Englewood, Colo.: Libraries Unlimited, 1996.

Shannon, Donna. "Tracking the Transition to a Flexible Access Library Program in Two Library Power Elementary Schools." *School Library Media Quarterly* 24 (Spring 1996): 155, 158–63.

Stripling, Barbara K. "Library Power: A Model for School Change." *School Library Media Quarterly* 25 (Summer 1997): 201–02.

Tallman, Julie and Shirley Tastad. Library Power: A Potent Agent for Change in Media Programs, *School Libraries Worldwide* 4 (January 1998): 33–49.

Tastad, Shirley and Julie Tallman. "Library Power: Vehicle for Change." *Knowledge Quest* 26 (January/February 1998): 17–23.

Useem, Elizabeth and Cati Coe. *Library Power in Philadelphia: Final Report from Seven Case Studies.* Philadelphia: Philadelphia Education Fund, 1997. (Available from Philadelphia Education Fund, Seven Benjamin Franklin Parkway, Suite 700, Philadelphia, PA 19103)

Additional information about the Library Power Initiative can be obtained from the office of the American Association of School Librarians, 1-800-545-2433, ext. 4386.

Appendix B
ICONnect
A technology initiative of the American Association of School Librarians, a division of the American Library Association

CONNECTING STUDENTS, LIBRARY MEDIA SPECIALISTS AND TEACHERS TO LEARNING USING THE INTERNET

In 1995 the American Association of School Librarians, realizing the potential of the Internet to impact teaching and learning, developed ICONnect, a national technology initiative. The association identified a need for professional development of library media specialists who would be able to connect teachers and students to learning using Internet technology and assume a leadership position in integrating Internet resources into the curriculum.

ICONnect has five components to support library media specialists and other educators in using the Internet to connect teachers and kids to learning: online courses, curriculum connections, minigrants, KidsConnect and FamiliesConnect. The ICONnect Web site can be found at http://www.ala.org/ICONN.

Free **online courses** are designed for school library media specialists who have basic knowledge of e-mail and a connection to the Internet for e-mail. As of May 1998, over 5,500 educators have taken them from all regions of the United States and from foreign countries. Delivered courses are archived on the Web for access any time, any place. The courses offer instruction in:

- Basic Internet awareness
- Curriculum integration using the Web
- Integrating the Internet into the elementary curriculum
- Developing content for a homepage
- Information literacy and Internet

- K–12 Internet issues
- Parents and children as learning partners together on the Internet
- Using Internet and Web search engines effectively
- Advanced Internet and Web search engines
- Clarification and redefinition of twenty-first century role of the school library media specialist
- Telecollaborative activities on the Net
- New trends in interactivity on the Web
- Navigating the World Wide Web

Curriculum Connections provides students and educators with the critical tools they need to evaluate web sites and showcase excellent Internet-based curriculum units. Curriculum Connections also hosts two electronic discussion lists for AASL members on the topics of curriculum integration using the Internet and technical Internet issues. These discussions facilitate collaboration and idea sharing among school librarians and complement the other ICONnect components by providing an open forum for discussion.

ICONnect awards **minigrants** to collaborative teams of AASL members and classroom teachers for outstanding projects that integrate Internet resources into the curriculum. Descriptions of the winning projects and the criteria for their evaluation are available on the ICONnect web site for educators to consult.

KidsConnect, ICONnect's question-answering, help and referral services for K–12 students, responded to more than 10,000 reference questions form its debut in April 1996 to May 1998. Operated in partnership with the Information Institute of Syracuse at Syracuse University, KidsConnect models the new national information literacy standards by contributing to the teaching of children how to access and use the information available on the Internet effectively and efficiently. KidsConnect is underwritten by Microsoft Corporation.

Over 215 volunteer school library media specialists from around the world are collaborating on KidsConnect to provide direct assistance to any K–12 student who is looking for resources for school or personal interests. Through e-mail, students contact the main KidsConnect address and receive a response from a volunteer library media specialist within two school days.

FamiliesConnect provides parents, grandparents, aunts, uncles, and other family members with the strategies and resources to effectively use the Internet with kids. Links to online courses, relevant Web sites, and other opportunities on the Internet are highlighted on the FamiliesConnect home page. Media specialists can use this page as a starting point or guide to reach out to parents and community members.

The ICONnect Publication Series provides print resources to support and extend the initiative, offering strategies, techniques and list of resources to integrate information processing skills and the Internet into the teaching and learning process. The series includes: Pam Berger, *Internet for Active Learners: Curriculum-Based Strategies for K.12* (Chicago, Ill.: ALA, 1998) and two booklets: *How to Connect to the Internet* and *Curriculum Connections on the 'Net.*

Appendix C
Statements and Policies

ALA
Library Bill of Rights

The American Library Association affirms that all libraries are forums for information and ideas, and that the following basic policies should guide their services.

I.   Books and other library resources should be provided for the interest, information, and enlightenment of all people of the community the library serves. Materials should not be excluded because of the origin, background, or views of those contributing to their creation.

II. Libraries should provide materials and information presenting all points of view on current and historical issues. Materials should not be proscribed or removed because of partisan or doctrinal disapproval.

III. Libraries should challenge censorship in the fulfillment of their responsibility to provide information and enlightenment.

IV. Libraries should cooperate with all persons and groups concerned with resisting abridgment of free expression and free access to ideas.

V.   A person's right to use a library should not be denied or abridged because of origin, age, background, or views.

VI. Libraries which make exhibit spaces and meeting rooms available to the public they serve should make such facilities available on an equitable basis, regardless of the beliefs or affiliations of individuals or groups requesting their use.

Adopted June 18, 1948.
amended February 2, 1961, and January 23, 1980,
inclusion of "age" reaffirmed January 23, 1996,
by the ALA Council.

ALA
Access to Resources and Services in the School Library Media Program
An Interpretation of the *Library Bill of Rights*

The school library media program plays a unique role in promoting intellectual freedom. It serves as a point of voluntary access to information and ideas and as a learning laboratory for students as they acquire critical thinking and problem solving skills needed in a pluralistic society. Although the educational level and program of the school necessarily shape the resources and services of a school library media program, the principles of the *Library Bill of Rights* apply equally to all libraries, including school library media programs.

School library media professionals assume a leadership role in promoting the principles of intellectual freedom within the school by providing resources and services that create and sustain an atmosphere of free inquiry. School library media professionals work closely with teachers to integrate instructional activities in classroom units designed to equip students to locate, evaluate, and use a broad range of ideas effectively. Through resources, programming, and educational processes, students and teachers experience the free and robust debate characteristic of a democratic society.

School library media professionals cooperate with other individuals in building collections of resources appropriate to the developmental and maturity levels of students. These collections provide resources which support curriculum and are consistent with the philosophy, goals, and objectives of the school district. Resources in school library media collections represent diverse points of view on current as well as historical issues.

While English is, by history and tradition, the customary language of the United States, the languages in use in any given community may vary. Schools serving communities in which other languages are used make efforts to accommodate the needs of students for whom English is a second language. To support these efforts, and to ensure equal access to resources and services, the school library media program provides resources which reflect the linguistic pluralism of the community.

Members of the school community involved in the collection development process employ educational criteria to select resources unfettered by their personal, political, social, or religious views. Students and educators served by the school library media program have access to resources and services free of constraints resulting from personal, partisan, or doctrinal disapproval. School library media professionals resist efforts by individuals to define what is appropriate for all students or teachers to read, view, or hear.

Major barriers between students and resources include: imposing age or grade level restrictions on the use of resources, limiting the use of interlibrary loan and access to electronic information, charging fees for information in specific formats, requiring permission from parents or teachers, establishing restricted shelves or closed collections, and labeling. Policies, procedures, and rules related to the use of resources and services support free and open access to information. The school board adopts policies that guarantee students access to a broad range of ideas. These include policies on collection development and procedures for the review of resources about which concerns have been raised. Such policies, developed by the persons in the school community, provide for a timely and fair hearing and assure that procedures are applied equitably to all expressions of concern. School library media professionals implement district policies and procedures in the school.

Adopted July 2, 1986;
amended January 10, 1990,
by the ALA Council.

ALA Confidentiality of Library Records

The members of the American Library Association,* recognizing the right to privacy of library users, believe that records held in libraries which connect specific individuals with specific resources, programs or services, are confidential and not to be used for purposes other than routine record keeping: i.e., to maintain access to resources, to assure that resources are available to users who need them, to arrange facilities, to provide resources for the comfort and safety of patrons, or to accomplish the purposes of the program or service. The library community recognizes that children and youth have the same rights to privacy as adults.

Libraries whose record keeping systems reveal the names of users would be in violation of the confidentiality of library record laws adopted in many states. School library media specialists are advised to seek the advice of counsel if in doubt about whether their record keeping systems violate the specific laws in their states. Efforts must be made within the reasonable constraints of budgets and school management procedures to eliminate such records as soon as reasonably possible.

With or without specific legislation, school library media specialists are urged to respect the rights of children and youth by adhering to the tenets expressed in the Confidentiality of Library Records Interpretation of the Library Bill of Rights and the ALA Code of Ethics.

*ALA Policy 52.4, 54.16

ALA
The Freedom to Read

The freedom to read is essential to our democracy. It is continuously under attack. Private groups and public authorities in various parts of the country are working to remove books from sale, to censor textbooks, to label "controversial" books, to distribute lists of "objectionable" books or authors, and to purge libraries. These actions apparently rise from a view that our national tradition of free expression is no longer valid; that censorship and suppression are needed to avoid the subversion of politics and the corruption of morals. We, as citizens devoted to the use of books and as librarians and publishers responsible for disseminating them, wish to assert the public interest in the preservation of the freedom to read.

We are deeply concerned about these attempts at suppression. Most such attempts rest on a denial of the fundamental premise of democracy: that the ordinary citizen, by exercising critical judgment, will accept the good and reject the bad. The censors, public and private, assume that they should determine what is good and what is bad for their fellow-citizens.

We trust Americans to recognize propaganda, and to reject it. We do not believe they need the help of censors to assist them in this task. We do not believe they are prepared to sacrifice their heritage of a free press in order to be "protected" against what others think may be bad for them. We believe they still favor free enterprise in ideas and expression.

We are aware, of course, that books are not alone in being subjected to efforts at suppression. We are aware that these efforts are related to a larger pattern of pressures being brought against education, the press, films, radio and television. The problem is not only one of actual censorship. The shadow of fear cast by these pressures leads, we suspect, to an even larger voluntary curtailment of expression by those who seek to avoid controversy.

Such pressure toward conformity is perhaps natural to a time of uneasy change and pervading fear. Especially when so many of our apprehensions are directed against an ideology, the expression of a dissident idea becomes a thing feared in itself, and we tend to move against it as against a hostile deed, with suppression.

And yet suppression is never more dangerous than in such a time of social tension. Freedom has given the United States the elasticity to endure strain. Freedom keeps open the path of novel and creative solutions, and enables change to come by choice. Every silencing of a heresy, every enforcement of an orthodoxy, diminishes the toughness and resilience of our society and leaves it the less able to deal with stress.

Now as always in our history, books are among our greatest instruments of freedom. They are almost the only means for making generally available ideas or manners of expression that can initially command only a small audience. They are the natural medium for the new idea and the untried voice from which come the original contributions to social growth. They are essential to the extended discussion which serious thought requires, and to the accumulation of knowledge and ideas into organized collections.

We believe that free communication is essential to the preservation of a free society and a creative culture. We believe that these pressures towards conformity present the danger of limiting the range and variety of inquiry and expression on which our democracy and our culture depend. We believe that every American community must jealously guard the freedom to publish and to circulate, in order to preserve its own freedom to read. We believe that publishers and librarians have a profound responsibility to give validity to that freedom to read by making it possible for the readers to choose freely from a variety of offerings.

The freedom to read is guaranteed by the Constitution. Those with faith in free people will stand firm on these constitutional guarantees of essential rights and will exercise the responsibilities that accompany these rights.

We therefore affirm these propositions:

1. It is in the public interest for publishers and librarians to make available the widest diversity of views and expressions, including those which are unorthodox or unpopular with the majority.

Creative thought is by definition new, and what is new is different. The bearer of every new thought is a rebel until that idea is refined and tested. Totalitarian systems attempt to maintain themselves in power by the ruthless suppression of any concept which challenges the established orthodoxy. The power of a democratic system to adapt to change is vastly strengthened by the freedom of its citizens to choose widely from among conflicting opinions offered freely to them. To stifle every nonconformist idea at birth would mark the end of the democratic process. Furthermore, only through the constant activity of weighing and selecting can the democratic mind attain the strength demanded by times like these. We need to know not only what we believe but why we believe it.

2. Publishers, librarians and booksellers do not need to endorse every idea or presentation contained in the books they make available. It would conflict with the public interest for them to establish their own political, moral or aesthetic views as a standard for determining what books should be published or circulated.

Publishers and librarians serve the educational process by helping to make available knowledge and ideas required for the growth of the mind and the increase of learning. They do not foster education by imposing as mentors the patterns of their own thought. The people should have the freedom to read and consider a broader range of ideas than those that may be held by any single librarian or publisher or government or church. It is wrong that what one can read should be confined to what another thinks proper.

3. It is contrary to the public interest for publishers or librarians to determine the acceptability of a book on the basis of the personal history or political affiliations of the author.

A book should be judged as a book. No art or literature can flourish if it is to be measured by the political views or private lives of its creators. No society of free people can flourish which draws up lists of writers to whom it will not listen, whatever they may have to say.

4. There is no place in our society for efforts to coerce the taste of others, to confine adults to the reading matter deemed suitable for adolescents, or to inhibit the efforts of writers to achieve artistic expression.

To some, much of modern literature is shocking. But is not much of life itself shocking? We cut off literature at the source if we prevent writers from dealing with the stuff of life. Parents and teachers have a responsibility to prepare the young to meet the diversity of experiences in life to which they will be exposed, as they have a responsibility to help them learn to think critically for themselves. These are affirmative responsibilities, not to be discharged simply by preventing them from reading works for which they are not yet prepared. In these matters taste differs, and taste cannot be legislated; nor can machinery be devised which will suit the demands of one group without limiting the freedom of others.

5. It is not in the public interest to force a reader to accept with any book the prejudgment of a label characterizing the book or author as subversive or dangerous.
The ideal of labeling presupposes the existence of individuals or groups with wisdom to determine by authority what is good or bad for the citizen. It presupposes that individuals must be directed in making up their minds about the ideas they examine. But Americans do not need others to do their thinking for them.

6. It is the responsibility of publishers and librarians, as guardians of the people's freedom to read, to contest encroachments upon that freedom by individuals or groups seeking to impose their own standards or tastes upon the community at large.
It is inevitable in the give and take of the democratic process that the political, the moral, or the aesthetic concepts of an individual or group will occasionally collide with those of another individual or group. In a free society individuals are free to determine for themselves what they wish to read, and each group is free to determine what it will recommend to its freely associated members. But no group has the right to take the law into its own hands, and to impose its own concept of politics or morality upon other members of a democratic society. Freedom is no freedom if it is accorded only to the accepted and the inoffensive.

7. It is the responsibility of publishers and librarians to give full meaning to the freedom to read by providing books that enrich the quality and diversity of thought and expression. By the exercise of this affirmative responsibility, they can demonstrate that the answer to a bad book is a good one, the answer to a bad idea is a good one.
The freedom to read is of little consequence when expended on the trivial; it is frustrated when the reader cannot obtain matter fit for that reader's purpose. What is needed is not only the absence of restraint, but the positive provision of opportunity for the people to read the best that has been thought and said. Books are the major channel by which the intellectual inheritance is handed down, and the principal means of its testing and growth. The defense of their

freedom and integrity, and the enlargement of their service to society, requires of all publishers and librarians the utmost of their faculties, and deserves of all citizens the fullest of their support.

We state these propositions neither lightly nor as easy generalizations. We here stake out a lofty claim for the value of books. We do so because we believe that they are good, possessed of enormous variety and usefulness, worthy of cherishing and keeping free. We realize that the application of these propositions may mean the dissemination of ideas and manners of expression that are repugnant to many persons. We do not state these propositions in the comfortable belief that what people read is unimportant. We believe rather that what people read is deeply important; that ideas can be dangerous; but that the suppression of ideas is fatal to a democratic society. Freedom itself is a dangerous way of life, but it is ours.

This statement was originally issued in May of 1953 by the Westchester Conference of the American Library Association and the American Book Publishers Council, which in 1970 consolidated with the American Educational Publishers Institute to become the Association of American Publishers.

Adopted June 25, 1953; revised January 28, 1972, January 16, 1991, by the ALA Council and the AAP Freedom to Read Committee.

A Joint Statement by: American Library Association and the Association of American Publishers

Subsequently Endorsed by:

American Booksellers Association

American Booksellers Foundation for Free Expression

American Civil Liberties Union

American Federation of Teachers AFL-CIO

Anti-Defamation League of B'nai B'rith

Association of American University Presses

Children's Book Council

Freedom to Read Foundation

International Reading Association

Thomas Jefferson Center for the Protection of Free Expression

National Association of College Stores

National Council of Teachers of English

PEN American Center

People for the American Way

Periodical and Book Association of America

Sexuality Information and Education Council
of the United States

Society of Professional Journalists

Women's National Book Association

The YWCA of the USA

ALA
Access to Electronic Information, Services, and Networks
An Interpretation of the *Library Bill of Rights*

INTRODUCTION

The world is in the midst of an electronic communications revolution. Based on its constitutional, ethical, and historical heritage, American librarianship is uniquely positioned to address the broad range of information issues being raised in this revolution. In particular, librarians address intellectual freedom from a strong ethical base and an abiding commitment to the preservation of the individual's rights.

Freedom of expression is an inalienable human right and the foundation for self-government. Freedom of expression encompasses the freedom of speech and the corollary right to receive information. These rights extend to minors as well as adults. Libraries and librarians exist to facilitate the exercise of these rights by selecting, producing, providing access to, identifying, retrieving, organizing, providing instruction in the use of, and preserving recorded expression regardless of the format or technology.

The American Library Association expresses these basic principles of librarianship in its *Code of Ethics* and in the *Library Bill of Rights* and its Interpretations. These serve to guide librarians and library governing bodies in addressing issues of intellectual freedom that arise when the library provides access to electronic information, services, and networks.

Issues arising from the still-developing technology of computer-mediated information generation, distribution, and retrieval need to be approached and regularly reviewed from a context of constitutional principles and ALA policies so that fundamental and traditional tenets of librarianship are not swept away.

Electronic information flows across boundaries and barriers despite attempts by individuals, governments, and private entities to channel or control it. Even so, many people, for reasons of technology, infrastructure, or socio-economic status do not have access to electronic information.

In making decisions about how to offer access to electronic information, each library should consider its mission, goals, objectives, cooperative agreements, and the needs of the entire community it serves.

THE RIGHTS OF USERS

All library system and network policies, procedures or regulations relating to electronic resources and services should be scrutinized for potential violation of user rights.

User policies should be developed according to the policies and guidelines established by the American Library Association, including Guidelines for the Development and Implementation of Policies, Regulations, and Procedures Affecting Access to Library Materials, Services and Facilities.

Users should not be restricted or denied access for expressing or receiving constitutionally protected speech. Users' access should not be changed without due process, including, but not limited to, formal notice and a means of appeal.

Although electronic systems may include distinct property rights and security concerns, such elements may not be employed as a subterfuge to deny users' access to information. Users have the right to be free of unreasonable limitations or conditions set by libraries, librarians, system administrators, vendors, network service providers, or others. Contracts, agreements, and licenses entered into by libraries on behalf of their users should not violate this right. Users also have a right to information, training and assistance necessary to operate the hardware and software provided by the library.

Users have both the right of confidentiality and the right of privacy. The library should uphold these rights by policy, procedure, and practice. Users should be advised, however, that because security is technically difficult to achieve, electronic transactions and files could become public.

The rights of users who are minors shall in no way be abridged.[1]

EQUITY OF ACCESS

Electronic information, services, and networks provided directly or indirectly by the library should be equally, readily and equitably accessible to all library users. American Library Association policies oppose the charging of user fees for the provision of information services by all libraries and information services that receive their major support from public funds (50.3; 53.1.14; 60.1; 61.1). It should be the goal of all libraries to develop policies concerning access to electronic resources in light of Economic Barriers to Information Access: an Interpretation of the Library Bill of Rights and Guidelines for the Development and Implementation of Policies, Regulations and Procedures Affecting Access to Library Materials, Services and Facilities.

INFORMATION RESOURCES AND ACCESS

Providing connections to global information, services, and networks is not the same as selecting and purchasing material for a library collection. Determining the accuracy or authenticity of electronic information may present special problems. Some information accessed electronically may not meet a library's selection or collection development policy. It is, therefore, left to each user to determine what is appropriate. Parents and legal guardians who are concerned about their children's use of electronic resources should provide guidance to their own children.

Libraries and librarians should not deny or limit access to information available via electronic resources because of its allegedly controversial content or because of the librarian's personal beliefs or fear of confrontation. Information retrieved or utilized electronically should be considered constitutionally protected unless determined otherwise by a court with appropriate jurisdiction.

Libraries, acting within their mission and objectives, must support access to information on all subjects that serve the needs or interests of each user, regardless of the user's age or the content of the material. Libraries have an obligation to provide access to government information available in electronic format. Libraries and librarians should not deny access to information solely on the grounds that it is perceived to lack value.

In order to prevent the loss of information, and to preserve the cultural record, libraries may need to expand their selection or collection development policies to ensure preservation, in appropriate formats, of information obtained electronically.

Electronic resources provide unprecedented opportunities to expand the scope of information available to users. Libraries and librarians should provide access to information presenting all points of view. The provision of access does not imply sponsorship or endorsement. These principles pertain to electronic resources no less than they do to the more traditional sources of information in libraries.[2]

Adopted by the ALA Council, January 24, 1996

Notes

[1]*See* Free Access to Libraries for Minors: An Interpretation of the Library Bill of Rights; Access to Resources and Services in the School Library Media Program: An Interpretation of the Library Bill of Rights; and Access for Children and Young People to Videotapes and Other Nonprint Formats: An Interpretation of the Library Bill of Rights.

[2]*See* Diversity in Collection Development: An Interpretation of the Library Bill of Rights.

See also Questions and Answers on Access to Electronic Information, Services and Networks: An Interpretation of the Library Bill of Rights.

AECT
Code of Ethics

PREAMBLE

1. The Code of Ethics contained herein shall be considered to be principles of ethics. These principles are intended to aid members individually and collectively in maintaining a high level of professional conduct.

2. The Professional Ethics Committee will build documentation of opinion (interpretive briefs or ramifications of intent) relating to specific ethical statements enumerated herein.

3. Opinions may be generated in response to specific cases brought before the Professional Ethics Committee.

4. Amplification and/or clarification of the ethical principles may be generated by the Committee in response to a request submitted by a member.

SECTION 1 - COMMITMENT TO THE INDIVIDUAL

In fulfilling obligations to the individual, the members:

1. Shall encourage independent action in an individual's pursuit of learning and shall provide access to varying points of view.

2. Shall protect the individual rights of access to materials of varying points of view.

3. Shall guarantee to each individual the opportunity to participate in any appropriate program.

4. Shall conduct professional business so as to protect the privacy and maintain the personal integrity of the individual.

5. Shall follow sound professional procedures for evaluation and selection of materials and equipment.

6. Shall make reasonable effort to protect the individual from conditions harmful to health and safety.

7. Shall promote current and sound professional practices in the use of technology in education.

8. Shall in the design and selection of any educational program or media seek to avoid content that reinforces or promotes gender, ethnic, racial, or religious stereotypes. Shall seek to encourage the development of programs and media that emphasize the diversity of our society as a multi-cultural community.

9. Shall refrain from any behavior that would be judged to be discriminatory, harassing, insensitive, or offensive and, thus, is in conflict with valuing and promoting each individuals integrity, rights, and opportunity within a diverse profession and society.

SECTION 2 - COMMITMENT TO SOCIETY

In fulfilling obligations to society, the member:

1. Shall honestly represent the institution or organization with which that person is affiliated, and shall take adequate precautions to distinguish between personal and institutional or organizational views.

2. Shall represent accurately and truthfully the facts concerning educational matters in direct and indirect public expressions.

3. Shall not use institutional or Associational privileges for private gain.

4. Shall accept no gratuities, gifts, or favors that might impair or appear to impair professional judgment, or offer any favor, service, or thing of value to obtain special advantage.

5. Shall engage in fair and equitable practices with those rendering service to the profession.

SECTION 3 - COMMITMENT TO THE PROFESSION

In fulfilling obligations to the profession, the member:

1. Shall accord just and equitable treatment to all members of the profession in terms of professional rights and responsibilities.

2. Shall not use coercive means to promise special treatment in order to influence professional decisions or colleagues.

3. Shall avoid commercial exploitation of that person's membership in the Association.

4. Shall strive continually to improve professional knowledge and skill and to make available to patrons and colleagues the benefit of that person's professional attainments.

5. Shall present honestly personal professional qualifications and the professional qualifications and evaluations of colleagues.

6. Shall conduct professional business through proper channels.

7. Shall delegate assigned tasks to qualified personnel. Qualified personnel are those who have appropriate training or credentials and/or who can demonstrate competency in performing the task.

8. Shall inform users of the stipulations and interpretations of the copyright law and other laws affecting the profession and encourage compliance.

9. Shall observe all laws relating to or affecting the profession; shall report, without hesitation, illegal or unethical conduct of fellow members of the profession to the AECT Professional Ethics Committee; shall participate in professional inquiry when requested by the Association.

AECT
Statement on Intellectual Freedom

The First Amendment to the Constitution of the United States is a cornerstone of our liberty, supporting our rights and responsibilities regarding free speech both written and oral.

The Association for Educational Communications and Technology believes this same protection applies also to the use of sound and image in our society.

Therefore, we affirm that:

Freedom of inquiry and access to information—regardless of the format or viewpoints of the presentation—are fundamental to the development or our society. These rights must not be denied or abridged because of age, sex, race, religion, national origin, or social or political views.

Children have the right to freedom of inquiry and access to information; responsibility for abridgement of that right is solely between an individual child and the parent(s) of that child.

The need for information and the interests, growth, and enlightenment of the user should govern the selection and development of educational media, not the age, sex, race, nationality, politics, or religious doctrine of the author, producer, or publisher.

Attempts to restrict or deprive a learner's access to information representing a variety of viewpoints must be resisted as a threat to learning in a free and democratic society. Recognizing that within a pluralistic society efforts to censor may exist, such challenges should be met calmly with proper respect for the beliefs of the challengers. Further, since attempts to censor sound and image material frequently arise out of misunderstanding of the rationale for using these formats, we shall attempt to help both user and censor to recognize the purpose and dynamics of communication in modern times regardless of the format.

The Association for Educational Communications and Technology is ready to cooperate with other persons or groups committed to resisting censorship or abridgement of free expression and free access to ideas and information.

Adopted by:
AECT Board of Directors
Kansas City
April 21, 1978

Appendix D
NSSE Schoolwide Goals
for Student Learning

Learning-to-Learn Skills
- Students make a commitment to creating quality work and striving for excellence
- Students use a variety of learning strategies, personal skills, and time management skills to enhance learning
- Students reflect on and evaluate their learning for the purpose of improvement

Expanding and Integrating Knowledge
- Students connect knowledge and experiences from different subject areas
- Students use what they already know to acquire new knowledge, develop new skills, and expand understanding
- Students demonstrate integrated knowledge and skills in applying multidisciplinary approaches to solving problems or completing skills

Communication Skills
- Students communicate with clarity, purpose and understanding of audience
- Students integrate the use of a variety of communication forms and use a wide range of communication skills
- Students recognize, analyze and evaluate various forms of communication

Thinking and Reasoning Skills
Critical Thinking, Problem-Solving, and Creative Thinking

- Students gather and use information effectively to gain new information and knowledge, classify and organize information, support inferences and justify conclusions appropriate to the context and audience

- Students utilize, evaluate and refine the use of multiple strategies to solve a variety of types of problems
- Students generate new and creative ideas by taking considered risks in a variety of contexts

Interpersonal Skills
- Students work with others in a variety of situations to set and achieve goals
- Students manage and evaluate their behavior as group members
- Students deal with disagreement and conflict caused by diversity of opinions and beliefs

Personal and Social Responsibility
- Students take responsibility for personal actions and act ethically (e.g., demonstrate honesty, fairness, integrity)
- Students respect themselves and others, and understand and appreciate the diversity and interdependence of all people
- Students demonstrate an understanding of and responsibility for global and environmental issues
- Students act as responsible citizens in the community, state and nation

Source: "Schoolwide Goals for Student Learning" based on the *Indicators of Schools of Quality (Vol 1: Schoolwide Indicators of Quality)*, 1997. National Study of School Evaluation, Schaumburg, IL.

Appendix E
Student Performance Assessment

WHAT IS ASSESSMENT?

Assessment is the process of collecting, analyzing, and reporting data. The Latin verb *assidere*—assess(us), meaning literally to sit down beside—is the root word, and over time assessment has come to mean the careful judgment from close observation that results from sitting down beside someone.[1] Assessment differs from evaluation, with a literal meaning of placing value; evaluation evokes a quantitative or judgmental quality. Evaluation usually occurs when students finish a task, whereas assessment goes beyond evaluation to include gathering information about student performance as they work as well as when they are finished. Assessment is also usually done with the student, while evaluation is done to the student's work.

Change in our understanding and expectations for assessment has evolved parallel to our changing understanding of learning. Current practices in teaching and learning have been greatly influenced by several theories, which in turn affect assessment strategies:

- *Constructivism* places the learner at the center of a dynamic learning process; the learner constructs knowledge rather than passively absorbing it

- An emerging perspective of learning as not necessarily a linear progression of discrete skills but as a *recursive process* involving the integration of skills and content knowledge

- *Learning styles* models characterize how individuals perceive information, manipulate and evaluate it, and apply their findings to solve problems or create new ideas

Assessment tasks often engage students in inquiry and production to communicate and demonstrate what they know. Teachers may evaluate student work based on the students' final product.

---

[1] *Assessment at Alverno College* (Milwaukee: Wisc.: Alverno College, 1985), p. 1.

The school library media specialist, however, is equally concerned with the processes of seeking, evaluating, and using information that students practice to arrive at the final product, whether it is a traditional paper, a multimedia production, an oral presentation, or another format. Strategies or techniques for assessing students' proficiency in the processes of information work are different from conventional evaluation techniques. As time permits, the school library media specialist can conduct "on-the-spot" assessment of students at work to obtain indicators of *how* the students are doing. In this context, assessment can be seen as part of the teaching process itself rather than as a separate task.

WHY ASSESS?

Assessment, in itself, is a vital learning experience that involves reflection and appraisal of learning. It is an integral part of the information literacy standards for student learning that encourages continual examination of both teaching and learning for improved student performance. The school library media specialist can work closely with teachers in developing assessment techniques and, as time allows, work individually with students to assess their performance. Not only does assessment benefit the student and teacher, the school library media specialist can also use assessment results in determining the program's strengths and weaknesses.

Assessment serves several purposes. First, students perform better when they can determine the goal or see models and know how their performance compares to a standard. "Students recognize that perfomance assessment is not just a grade given at the end of work, but also a road map showing the path they must travel to improve their learning" (Sperling and Malwick, p. 39). Assessment in itself is a learning experience that involves reflection and appraisal of learning.

The NCTM Standards Addendum on Assessment identifies four purposes for assessment; these four purposes are relevant for the library media specialist's roles in assessment as well:

- *Improve student growth.* How is each student progressing in relation to the goals that have been set and agreed upon? Giving the student ongoing information and feedback based on assessment as they work can help improve student growth.

- *Improve instruction.* What changes or adjustments can be made in teaching to improve learning? Information from the assessment process can help improve future instruction.

- *Recognize accomplishment.* How does this student's performance compare with overall expectations? Giving information from the assessment processes to students and parents is one way to recognize accomplishment.

- *Modify or improve the program.* How well is the program working in relation to the goals and expectations of all the students? Educators can look at overall student performance to help determine the program's success and use assessment results to modify or improve the program.

THE ASSESSMENT PROCESS

Assessment should be ongoing, measuring student performance throughout the process of learning. Several important questions must be addressed as school library media specialists and teachers plan their assessment strategies:

- Does the assessment method measure what it says it measures?

- Are the scoring criteria clear, descriptive, and explicitly related to school, district, or national goals and standards?

- Does the scoring system enable a reliable yet adequately fine discrimination of degrees of work quality?

- Is the task being assessed a challenging one? Is it an appropriate stretch for students?

- Does the task being assessed reflect real-world challenges, contexts, and constraints? (Wiggins, p. 20)

School library media specialists collaborate with teachers in assessment of student performance in several ways. They can design and use assessment techniques to monitor students' information-seeking processes. They can recommend and model a variety of communication products including Web pages, interactive electronic presentations, video, and photography, and help students learn how to create them as well as to determine which format is most appropriate for the intended use. As often or as much as schedules allow, school library media specialists can assess student performance, both in formative assessment as students are working on projects and in summative assessment of final products.

ASSESSMENT STRATEGIES

Assessment may take place in the classroom, in the media center, and even in the students' homes. Both the assessment tool and the results of the assessment can be captured in electronic form, making their uses even more flexible for the school library media specialist, the teacher, and the student.

Several types of assessment tools can be used. Following are some assessment strategies and examples that are often used in school library media programs.

Checklist Strategy

A checklist is given to students at the beginning of a research activity so that the criteria are clear from the beginning. A checklist is simply a guide that helps students attend to all aspects of the research process. It can include elements for the process as well as the product. The following example of a checklist guides research into a question or issues of particular interest to the student.

Checklist Example

Instructions: the student checks off (or gets the teacher or school library media specialist's signature) as each of the following phases of the research process are completed.

_____ 1. I chose a topic on _____ that is interesting to me.

_____ 2. I listed questions about my topic that I want to answer.

_____ 3. I found information about my topic in at least two kinds of resources.

_____ 4. I took notes to answer my questions. My notes give important and complete information.

_____ 5. I used my notes to write sentences about my topic.

_____ 6. I prepared my oral report using my notes.

_____ 7. I shared my report with another class.

_____ 8. I assessed how well I did each step based on what the research project's instructions said.

Rubric Strategy

A rubric is a scaled set of criteria that clearly defines for the student and the teacher what a range of acceptable and unacceptable performances looks like. Its purpose is to provide a description of successful performance. A critical feature of rubrics is language that describes rather than labels performance. Evaluative words, like "better," "more often," and "excellent" do not appear in rubrics. Instead, the language must precisely define actions in terms of what the student actually does to demonstrate skill or proficiency at that level. Following are examples of rubrics for process and product.

Rubric Example for Process

Demonstrated indicator of student performance: integrates new information into one's own knowledge.

- Novice: puts information together without processing it.
- Apprentice: integrates information from a variety of sources to create meaning that is relevant to own prior knowledge and draws conclusions.
- Expert: integrates information to create meaning that connects with prior personal knowledge, draws conclusions, and provides details and supportive evidence.

Source: Adapted from Callison 1998, p. 43.

Rubric Example for Product

Rubric for Assessing Slide Shows

Quality of Content
  3 Message is clear to the audience; all slides support main idea
  2 Audience is unsure of message; some slides support main idea, other slides detract from message
  1 No clear message; details on slides have little or nothing to do with the main idea

Organization
  3 Audience understands organization of slides as a whole; order of slides makes sense to audience

2 Slides are somewhat organized; some slides seem confusing or out of order

1 Audience is confused as to how slides tie together; organization of slide show interferes with message

Style

3 Slide design has appropriate transitions, graphics, sound, and color; consistent background and fonts used throughout slide show

2 Slide design has inconsistent use of appropriate transitions, graphics, sound, and color; more than one background and font used in slide show

1 Slide design's choice of transitions, graphics, sound and color seem "random" to audience; variety of background and fonts appears to be used only for variety's sake

Mechanics

3 Slide show runs smoothly; written text has been carefully checked; spoken parts are expressive and easily understood by audience

2 Parts of slide show do not work the way they are intended to; written text has several noticeable errors; some spoken parts are not clear, not interesting, or have background noise

1 Slide show doesn't run or is missing parts; written text has many errors; spoken parts are hard to hear or understand

Source: Adapted and reprinted with permission from "Rubric for Assessing Kid Pics Slide Shows," Heidi Ersten and Adele Kehoe, September, 1995.

Conferencing Strategy

Conferencing can take place on several levels, from very informal to formal with a sit-down conference and a hard copy report on the session. Conferencing about research can be formal or informal. As students research, the teacher or school library media specialist can inquire about progress by asking questions specific to the students' task, so that specific feedback and guidance can be provided to them. More formal conferencing can occur at the end of a teaching sequence where students are asked questions that engage them in reflecting on their work, identifying what went well, and determining what they would change given the opportunity.

Conferencing Example

Both formal and informal conferencing can help students and teachers assess progress. As students work, the teacher or library media specialist can move from student to student to inquire about progress. Important in the conferencing is that a simple "How are you doing?" followed by "OK" is not adequate. The questions in an informal conference must be more specific in order to really focus attention on the research process. So, in informal conferencing, the question may be, "What is your topic? What research questions have you written about it?" or "What sources of information have you found?" or "How are you organizing your notes?" or "How are you keeping track of your resources for your bibliography?" Questions like these call for the student to explain some aspect of the research process.

Formal conferencing may be an appropriate assessment technique especially at the end of a research activity, so that students review their experience to see what they have learned about the process. Every student is scheduled to conference with either the teacher or the library media specialist. A schedule of questions for a formal conference might look like this:

- How did you find your information?
- Can you think of any problems you encountered as you did your research? What was hard about doing research? Where did you get stuck?
- What was most interesting to you about doing this research project?

These formal conferences not only monitor these students' learning; when patterns emerge as all students' responses are reviewed, they give insight into how teaching could be improved for future students.

Source: Jean Donham, *Assessing Information Processes and Products* (McHenry, Ill.: Follett Software Company, 1998).

Journaling Strategy

The intent of the journaling assessment strategy is to cause students to focus, at least briefly, on the research process as well as the content of their research. Their brief entries into a journal can give the teacher and the school library media specialist a sense of how students are doing: this information may suggest mini-lessons that need to be taught next. Journal entries also help the students at the beginning of the subsequent session to know precisely where they need to begin.

Journaling Example

Students respond to reflection prompts at different phases of the information search process. For instance, when they are locating and evaluating different resources for their information, the teacher or school library media specialist could ask students to respond to the following reflection prompt: "Which resource(s) appear to be most useful for your information need? Please explain." The student's reflections become part of the inquiry process, but they also can help the school library media specialist determine ways to modify and improve instruction.

Portfolio Strategy

Portfolio assessment is a cumulative process in which samples of student work are collected over a period of time to demonstrate the learning that has taken place. The student's portfolio must contain deliberate compilations, not casual collections, of items. The portfolio is a documentation of student growth based on the student's learning goals established at the beginning of the portfolio compilation. The student's own reflection on his or her work is also an important aspect of portfolio assessment.

Portfolio compilations can vary in their content and form; for example, they may be arranged chronologically, by topic, or by format. The critical requirement of the portfolio assessment tool is that the content of the portfolio matches the student learning goals. Formats can include learning logs, videotapes of student performance, or samples of student written work, speeches, artwork, electronic presentations, or interactive hypermedia stacks. Many of these student products reflect application, synthesis, and communication of information they have found.

While the classroom teacher has primary responsibility for portfolio assessment, the school library media specialist can contribute both to the development of criteria for evaluation of portfolio items and to the design of the assessment tasks as well as assist the student in his or her critical analysis, as time allows.

Portfolio Example

Over the course of a school year, students in an eighth-grade language arts class work on six major inquiry-based learning activities. Each activity results in three items: a student work progress report, a product, and a self-assessment. All three items are saved in the student's working portfolio.

For the year's end evaluation and parent/student/teacher conferences, the student selects three of the learning activity products to include in the assessment portfolio. The student, with help from the teacher or school library media specialist, critically reviews each portfolio item based on the criteria established for the learning activity and on the learning goals they set at the beginning of the term. The student then writes a statement of rationale for the item's inclusion in the portfolio. Selected items are those that the student believes best demonstrate the knowledge and skills gained in all phases of the inquiry process, from formulating a question to the final evaluation of the product and process.

By planning with teachers, school library media specialists can assist in expanding assignments and creating a learning environment that allows authentic learning activities to become possible. School library media specialists also provide an additional perspective that may encourage students to improve their performance.

REFERENCES

Barton, James, and Angelo Collins, eds. *Portfolio Assessment: A Handbook for Educators.* Menlo Park, Calif.: Addison-Wesley, 1997.

Callison, Daniel. "Authentic Assessment." *School Library Media Activities Monthly* 14, no. 5 (January 1998): 42–43, 50.

———. "Portfolio." *School Library Media Activities Monthly* 14, no. 2 (October 1997): 42–44.

———. "The Potential for Portfolio Assessment," *School Library Media Annual* (1993): 30–39.

Donham, Jean. *Assessing Information Processes and Products* (working title). McHenry, Ill.: Follett Software Company, 1998.

Grover, Robert. "Assessing Information Skills Instruction." *Reference Librarian* no. 44 (1994): 173–89.

Harada, Violet H., and Joan Yoshina. "The Missing Link: One Elementary School's Journey with Assessment." *School Library Media Activities Monthly* (March 1998): 25–29.

Hart, Diane, ed. *Authentic Assessment: A Handbook for Educators.* Menlo Park, Calif.: Addison-Wesley, 1994.

Herman, Joan. *A Practical Guide to Alternative Assessment.* Alexandria, Va.: Association for Supervision and Curriculum Development, 1992.

Huck, Charlotte S. "Literature Based Reading Programs: A Retrospective." *The New Advocate* (Winter 1996): 23–33.

Jacobs, Heidi Hayes. *Mapping the Big Picture: Integrating Curriculum and Assessment K–12.* Alexandria, Va.: Association for Supervision and Curriculum Development, 1997.

Kuhlthau, Carol Collier, ed. *Assessment and the School Library Media Center.* Englewood, Colo.: Libraries Unlimited, 1994.

Marzano, Robert J., Debra Pickering, and Jay McTighe. *Assessing Student Outcomes: Performance Assessment Using the Dimensions of Learning Model.* Alexandria, Va.: Association for Supervision and Curriculum Development, 1993.

McLaughlin, Maureen. *Portfolios in Education.* Newark, Del.: International Reading Association, 1996.

Sperling, Doris H., and Carolyn J. Mahalak, "Using Performance Assessment to Enhance Student's Learning." *Journal of Staff Development* 14, no. 3 (Summer 1993): 39.

Stripling, Barbara K. "Assessment of Student Performance: The Fourth Step in the Instructional Design Process." In *Assessment and the School Library Media Center,* edited by Carol C. Kuhlthau. Englewood, Colo.: Libraries Unlimited, 1994, 77–85.

Wiggins, Grant. "Practicing What We Preach in Designing Authentic Assessments." *Educational Leadership* 54, no. 4 (December 1996–January 1997): 18–25.

Appendix F
Contributors

AASL/AECT Vision Committee

Chairperson: Elizabeth L. (Betty) Marcoux
Head Librarian, Rincon/University Library
Adjunct Faculty, School of Information Resources
  and Library Science
University of Arizona
Tucson, Arizona

Writer: Delia Neuman
Associate Professor, College of Library and Information Services
University of Maryland
College Park, Maryland

Coordinator: Marilyn Miller
Professor Emeritus, Department of Library
  and Information Studies
University of North Carolina—Greensboro
Greensboro, North Carolina

Elizabeth M. (Betty) Bankhead
Library Media Specialist, Cherry Creek High School
Englewood, Colorado

Daniel D. Barron
Professor and School Library Media Program Coordinator,
  College of Library and Information Science
University of South Carolina
Columbia, South Carolina

Melvin Bowie (deceased)
Associate Professor and General Coordinator, Instructional
  Technology Program, College of Education
University of Georgia
Athens, Georgia

William J. Burns
Vice President of Sales and Marketing,
  Phoenix/BFA Educational Media/Coronet MTI
St. Louis, Missouri

Edward P. Caffarella
Professor, College of Education
University of Northern Colorado
Greeley, Colorado

Ricki L. Chowning
Director of Technology and REMC 7 Services, Ottawa Area
    Intermediate School District
Holland, Michigan

Carol Fox
Library Media Specialist, May Watts Elementary School
Naperville, Illinois

Paula Galland
Library Media Specialist, Brunswick High School
Brunswick, Georgia

Marybeth Green
Library Media Specialist, Walzem Elementary School
San Antonio, Texas

Dianne McAfee Hopkins
Associate Professor and School Library Media Coordinator,
    School of Library and Information Studies
University of Wisconsin—Madison
Madison, Wisconsin

Pamela K. Kramer
Pamela K. Kramer & Assoc., Inc.
Wauconda, Illinois

Carol Kroll
Director, Nassau School Library System
Greenvale, New York

Frances M. McDonald
Professor, Library Media Education Department
Mankato State University
Mankato, Minnesota

Mary J. (Meb) Norton
Director of Libraries, Metairie Park Country Day School
Metairie, Louisiana

Barbara K. Stripling
Library Power Director, Public Education Foundation
Chattanooga, Tennessee

Julie A. Walker
Executive Director, American Association of School Librarians
Chicago, Illinois

Ann Carlson Weeks
Director, Department of Libraries and Information Services,
    Chicago Public Schools
Chicago, Illinois

Linda L. Wolcott
Associate Professor, Department of Instructional Technology
Utah State University
Logan, Utah

Stanley D. Zenor
Executive Director, Association for Educational
    Communications and Technology
Washington, D. C.

AASL/AECT IMPLEMENTATION COMMITTEE

Coordinator: Marilyn Miller
Professor Emeritus, Library Science/Educational
    Technology Department
University of North Carolina—Greensboro
Greensboro, North Carolina

Don Adcock
Director, Library Power Program, American
    Association of School Librarians
Chicago, Illinois

Elizabeth M. (Betty) Bankhead
Library Media Specialist, Cherry Creek High School
Englewood, Colorado

Daniel D. Barron
Professor and School Library Media Program Coordinator,
    College of Library and Information Science
University of South Carolina
Columbia, South Carolina

Jim Bennett
Library Media Specialist, Shoreham-Wading River Schools
Shoreham, New York

Melvin Bowie (deceased)
Associate Professor and Graduate Coordinator, Instructional
    Technology Program, College of Education
University of Georgia
Athens, Georgia

William J. Burns
Vice President of Sales and Marketing,
    Phoenix/BFA Educational Media/Coronet MTI
St. Louis, Missouri

Ruth Catalano
Director, Instructional Materials, Washington
    Elementary School District
Phoenix, Arizona

Judith Gray
Library Media Specialist, Nottingham High School
Syracuse, New York

Robert Gray
Professor, Department of AV Communications
Kutztown University
Kutztown, Pennsylvania

Elsie C. Husom
Director of Media Technology, Brainerd Public Schools
Brainerd, Minnesota

Barbara Jeffus
School Library Consultant, California Department
    of Education
Sacramento, California

Jane P. Klasing
Director of Learning Resources (retired),
	Broward County School Board
Miami, Florida

Elizabeth L. (Betty) Marcoux
Head Librarian, Rincon/University Library
Adjunct Faculty, School of Information Resources
	and Library Science
University of Arizona
Tucson, Arizona

Delia Neuman
Associate Professor, College of Library and Information Services
University of Maryland
College Park, Maryland

Marjorie L. Pappas
Associate Professor and Coordinator of
	School Library Media Studies
University of Northern Iowa
Cedar Falls, Iowa

Barbara K. Stripling
Library Power Director, Public Education Foundation
Chattanooga, Tennessee

Ruth Toor
Library Media Specialist, Southern Boulevard School
Chatham, New Jersey

Stanley D. Zenor
Executive Director, Association for Educational
	Communications and Technology
Washington, D. C.

DELPHI STUDY PARTICIPANTS

Note: Participants are listed with the titles and affiliations they held
at the time of their participation.

Mary Alice Anderson
Library Media Specialist, Winona Middle School
Winona, Minnesota

Judi Varnai Aronson
Principal, PS 261 Campus,
    New York Public Schools
Brooklyn, New York

Susan H. Bannon
Director, Learning Resources Center
Associate Professor, Library Media
Auburn University
Auburn, Alabama

Sherie Bargar
Specialist, Media, School Board of Broward County
Fort Lauderdale, Florida

Donna J. Baumbach
Professor, College of Education
University of Central Florida
Orlando, Florida

Pam Berger
Library Media Specialist, Byram Hills High School
Armonk, New York

Kay Bland
Director of Instructional Media and Technology, Pulaski
    County Special School District
Little Rock, Arkansas

Sandra Block
Instructional Supervisor, Library Media Services,
    Miami-Dade County Public Schools
Miami, Florida

Brenda Brown
Library Director, Branson School
Ross, California

William Burns
Vice President of Sales and Marketing,
    Phoenix/BFA Educational Media/Coronet MTI
St. Louis, Missouri

Carolyn Cain
Interim Director, Library and Technology,
    Madison Metropolitan School District
Madison, Wisconsin

David Carr
Associate Professor and Chair, Library and Information
    Studies Department, School of Communication,
    Information and Library Studies
Rutgers University
New Brunswick, New Jersey

Kim Carter
Director of Information and Technology, Souhegan High School
Amherst, New Hampshire

Deborah Roberts Coleman
Director of Media Services, Barnwell Elementary School
Barnwell, South Carolina

Francene C. Costello
Director, Southern Westchester BOCES School Library System
Elmsford, New York

Greg Drake
Coordinator of Instructional Technology, Technology Office,
    Fayette County Public Schools
Lexington, Kentucky

Eliza T. Dresang
Associate Professor, School of Information Studies
Florida State University
Tallahassee, Florida

Su Eckhardt
Media Coordinator, Smoky Hill High School
Aurora, Colorado

Michael B. Eisenberg
Professor and Director, ERIC Clearinghouse on
    Information & Technology
Syracuse University
Syracuse, New York

Joseph R. Gotchy
Social Studies Teacher, Thomas Jefferson High School
Auburn, Washington

Gary Hartzell
Associate Professor, College of Education
University of Nebraska at Omaha
Omaha, Nebraska

Ken Haycock
Professor and Director, School of Library, Archival,
    and Information Studies
University of British Columbia
Vancouver, British Columbia

Rod Hevland
Library Media Specialist, Whitford Middle School
Beaverton, Oregon

Margaret Ishler
Professor and Chair, Department of Curriculum and Instruction
University of Northern Iowa
Cedar Falls, Iowa

Frances F. Jacobson
University Laboratory High School Librarian
University of Illinois at Urbana-Champaign
Champaign, Illinois

Mary James
Assistant Principal, Grandville High School
Grandville, Michigan

M. Ellen Jay
Library Media Specialist, Damascus Elementary School
Silver Spring, Maryland

Judy Jerome
Coordinator, OCM BOCES School Library System
Syracuse, New York

Doug Johnson
District Media Supervisor, Mankato Public Schools
Mankato, Minnesota

Phyllis Lacroix
Professor and Acquisitions Librarian
St. Cloud State University
St. Cloud, Minnesota

Diana Schott Lincks
Superintendent of Schools, Pineville Independent Schools
Pineville, Kentucky

Deborah Little
Associate Professor, Department of Instructional Support
    and Programs, College of Education
Alabama State University
Montgomery, Alabama

David V. Loertscher
Professor, School of Library and Information Science
San Jose State University
San Jose, California

Jacqueline C. Mancall
Professor, College of Information Studies
Drexel University
Philadelphia, Pennsylvania

Joseph Mattie
Consultant, State Department of Education, Division of Library
    Development, New York State Library
Albany, New York

Kay Maynard
Library Media Specialist, Canton High School
Canton, Illinois

Joy H. McGregor
Assistant Professor, School of Library and
    Information Studies
Texas Woman's University
Denton, Texas

Inabeth Miller
President, E. T. 3
Livermore, California

Sue H. Moeschl
Director of Information Services, Carmel Clay Schools
Carmel, Indiana

Paula K. Montgomery
Publisher, *School Library Media Activities Monthly*
Baltimore, Maryland

Marjorie L. Pappas
Associate Professor and Coordinator of School
    Library Media Studies
University of Northern Iowa
Cedar Falls, Iowa

Lotsee Patterson
Associate Professor, School of Library and
    Information Studies
University of Oklahoma
Norman, Oklahoma

Sheila Salmon
Senior Vice-President, New Visions for Public Schools Fund
    for New York City Public Education
New York, New York

Pat Scales
Library Media Specialist, Greenville Middle School
Greenville, South Carolina

Judi Shirley
Elementary Principal, Chattanooga School for the
    Arts and Sciences
Chattanooga, Tennessee

Carol Mann Simpson
Library Automation Facilitator, Library Technology Office,
    Mesquite Independent School District
Mesquite, Texas

Susan Snider
Education Consultant, Research and Innovation Unit,
    Division of Program Support, New Hampshire State
    Department of Education
Concord, New Hampshire

Pam Spencer
Coordinator of Library Services, Fairfax County Public Schools
Annandale, Virginia

Barbara K. Stripling
Library Power Director, Public Education Foundation
Chattanooga, Tennessee

Keith Swigger
Dean and Professor, School of Library and Information Studies
Texas Woman's University
Denton, Texas

Nancy P. Thomas
Assistant Professor, School of Library and
    Information Management
Emporia State University
Emporia, Kansas

Philip M. Turner
Dean, School of Library and Information Studies
University of Alabama
Tuscaloosa, Alabama

Dawn P. Vaughn
Library Program Specialist, Fairfax County Public Schools
Annandale, Virginia

Idella Washington
Library Media Specialist, Crocker Elementary School
New Orleans, Louisiana

Gary G. Wehlage
Professor, Department of Curriculum and Instruction
University of Wisconsin—Madison
Madison, Wisconsin

Janie B. Whaley
Library Media Specialist, Floyd Central Junior–Senior High School
Floyds Knobs, Indiana

Merchuria Chase Williams
Coordinator of Media Services, Instructional Services Center,
    Atlanta Public Schools
Atlanta, Georgia

INFORMATION POWER EDITORIAL TASK FORCE

Kay Bland
Director of Instructional Technology, Pulaski County Special
    School District
Little Rock, Arkansas

Jean Donham
Assistant Professor, University of Iowa School of Library and
    Information Science
Iowa City, Iowa

Vi Harada
Associate Professor, University of Hawaii, Library and Information
    Science Program
Honolulu, Hawaii

Elsie Husom
Media/Technology Director, Brainerd Public Schools
Brainerd, Minnesota

FINANCIAL CONTRIBUTORS

Honor Roll   ($1000+)

Individuals
Jim Bennett
Hilda and M. Ellen Jay
Retta Patrick

Affiliates
Illinois School Library Media Association
Kansas Association of School Librarians
    (in honor of Ruth Bell)
North Carolina Association of School Librarians
South Carolina Association of School Librarians
Virginia Educational Media Association

Organizations
Baker & Tyler Books
CTB Macmillan/McGraw-Hill Publishing

Encyclopaedia Britannica Educational Corporation
Gaylord Bros.
Media Flex, Inc.
NewsBank, Inc.
R. R. Bowker
Random House
SIRS

Sustaining Contributors ($200–$500)

Individuals
Dale Brown
Tina Craven
Clara Hoover

Affiliates
Alaska Association of School Librarians
Arizona State Library Association, School Library Media Division
Nevada Library Association, School & Children's Division
New England Media Association
  (in memory of Rheta Clark)
Educational Media Association of New Jersey
Oregon Educational Media Association
Texas Association of School Librarians
Wisconsin Educational Media Association
  (in honor of Carolyn Cain)

Organizations
ABC-CLIO
Bantam Doubleday Dell
Brodart Company
Follett Book/Follett Software Companies
HiWillow Research & Publishing
  (in memory of Carolyn Whitenack)
Pleasant Company
Weston Woods

Contributors ($25–$200)

AASL Past Presidents
Rebecca Bingham
Dorothy Blake

Dawn Heller
Marjorie Horowitz
    (in honor of Frances Henne)
Winona Jones
Judith King
Jean Lowrie
Jacqueline Mancall
Marilyn Miller
Ruth Toor

Individuals
Kay Bland
Mildred Lee
Harriet Selverstone

Affiliates
California Library Media Educators Association
Connecticut Educational Media Association
Maine Educational Media Association
Massachusetts School Library Media Association
New Hampshire Educational Media Association
Rhode Island Educational Media Association
    (in honor of Linda Aldrich)
Tennessee Association of School Librarians
Vermont Educational Media Association

Organizations
Association for Educational Communications and Technology
Charles W. Clark, Inc.
Holiday House
Library Learning Resources, Inc.
University of Alabama/SLIS

PRESIDENTS OF THE AMERICAN ASSOCIATION OF SCHOOL LIBRARIANS, 1993–99

Blanche Woolls: 1993–94
Jacqueline C. Mancall: 1994–95
David V. Loertscher: 1995–96
Barbara K. Stripling : 1996–97
Ken Haycock: 1997–98
Sharon Coatney: 1998–99

PRESIDENTS OF THE ASSOCIATION FOR EDUCATIONAL COMMUNICATIONS AND TECHNOLOGY, 1993–99

Addie Kinsinger: 1993–94
Kent Gustafson: 1994–95
Lynn Milet: 1995–96
William J. Burns: 1996–97
Franz Frederick: 1997–98
Robert A. Harrell: 1998–99

Maggie Jones, graduate student in the Department of Instructional Technology at Utah State University, and Linda Zeoli, graduate student in the College of Library and Information Services at the University of Maryland, also contributed substantially to the development of this material.

Index